Parallels

in

Autocratic Leadership

*"Power tends to corrupt,
and absolute power corrupts absolutely."*
(Lord Acton, British politician and historian)

Wolfgang Mack PhD

August 2018

Parallels in Autocratic Leadership

By Wolfgang Mack PhD

Published by WAMFAM Press
1301 Spring Street, Suite 28H
Seattle WA, 98104

Images by Wolfgang Mack
or in the public domain

ISBN-13: 978-1726344067
ISBN-10: 172-6344061
BISAC: Politics, Dictatorships, History

Printed in the USA

Also by this Author:
   "Memories and Lessons
    of my young life in Wartime Germany"
   "The Phases of Our Lives"
   "In Search of a New Morality"

Prologue

National Leader: *a person of great integrity and vision about his Nation's goals, who can choose his objectives well, and after hearing all sides can carry his determinations decisively into action by connecting the institutions and operations of government, within the rule of Law.* (after Frederick North, Prime Minister of Great Britain, 1770 to 1782)

Autocrat: *one who has undisputed political influence or power.* (per Merriam Webster)

Demagogue: *A politician who exploits people's prejudices and fears to gain power with false claims and promises.* {New World Dictionary)

Dictator: *one ruling in absolute power and often in oppressive ways.* (per Webster New Dictionary)

Fascist: *A follower of a political philosophy characterized by authoritarian views and a strong central government suppressing opposing opinions.* (per Webster New Dictionary)

Leaders of nations have the chance to make history. Some do it well, many are just as well forgotten. Our history books tell us how well the Leaders have done in the affairs of state, what they should have done, and what will condemn them for their failures.

But how well have they done for their citizens? Obviously, whatever Leaders do, or not do, will deeply affect the lives of their nation's 'ordinary people', especially when a Leader is using raw power to force his own ideologies on his citizens, thus turning into a dictator. This is what happened to the Portuguese under Salazar, to the Spaniards under Franco, to the Italians under Mussolini and, of course, to the Germans under Hitler, and to other Nations since.

We do expect a politician to have a vision for his country, and to convey his vision to the people. But all politicians who have become dictators have one thing in common - a 'messianic belief' that only they know what ails their countries, and only they know how to fix it. However, they will only succeed if they also have the ability to transfer their messianic belief to a large enough group of followers carefully selected for their readiness to be led. The demagogues who are the most successful in achieving this 'belief transfer' are those with the gift of fiery rhetoric.

Once they have a large enough group of enthusiastic followers they can make them do the dirty work to secure them in their sole leadership. From that point on, all they need to do to maintain their absolute power is such an ideologically inspired following willing to take to the streets with violence to subdue the ordinary people.

But no politician can become a dictator as long as his country's institutions are functioning well, and as long as people can freely talk to each other. This is why all aspiring dictators need to go after the free press and why they will make judges beholden to them.

Whatever occasional good may come from dictatorships they will always end up causing immeasurable harm, start wars and eventually lead to economic collapse. Once the dictator is gone the historians will step up to give us an account of how he managed to take absolute control over his country's government and what this has done to his own and to other nations.

It is one thing to present the 'big picture' of what a dictatorship is all about and the disasters it always creates. But what about all the 'ordinary people' who had to live through a dictatorship? How did they cope with oppression and persecution? How does an 'ordinary person' deal with the dilemma when his own beliefs are different from the way he is now forced to live? Without the personal experience what it means to live under a dictatorship one can only contemplate it in the abstract, but it is only the personal experience that can convey the entire enormity of the damage done to a Nation by its dictator.

As a minimum, the result of dictatorship will be great spiritual and also physical discomfort, having to weigh over and over again the 'pros and cons' of resisting the dictator's demands or accepting them as inevitable. In an environment of personal freedom these decisions would be made based on a person's character. Under the threat of persecution, guidance by 'character' will often have to be replaced by acquiescence, by a pragmatic weighing of benefits versus dire consequences.

Life under a dictatorship will deeply affect the very character of ordinary citizens. It can lead to permanent emotional and spiritual damage, or in the best case to a renewed hope for a better world.

Personal accounts of what actual people experience living under a dictatorship are perhaps the most effective way to convey the seriousness of letting politicians gain too much control over their nations. There are three stories to be told here - one of a boy growing up under a long gone dictator who had not been stopped in time, then of several modern-day dictatorships in our Western World, and finally about a present day demagogue who can still be stopped before potentially dragging our country into the abyss of dictatorship - but only if we take action in time to prevent history from repeating itself.

Every Demagogue is a potential Dictator

ONE

GERMANY'S DESCENT INTO DICTATORSHIP

"This then is the curse of one foul deed,
that it will always have to be followed by
new ones,
in a never ending cycle of violence."
From Friedrich Schiller's Epic "Wallenstein"

How I saw it as a young Boy.

Every morning my buddy Helmut would ring our door bell to pick me up for our ten minute walk to school. Still chewing on my slice of dark bread I shouldered my backpack, and off we went to our next stop to pick up our friend Gunter to join us.

As we were waiting for him to come down, a woman came out from his apartment building, whispered to us that "they were taken last night", and then hurried away. Helmut and I looked at each other, with disbelief, shock, fear written all over our faces. We knew what this meant - we had heard rumors often enough about people disappearing in the middle of the night, never to be seen again.

But now it had happened right here, to our best friend and his family. Helmut started to cry. Shaken we went on our way to school.

Without our friend Gunter.

The war was in its third year. Up to now we had seen little of it, except that food had become more scarce and more soldiers were dying. My two older brothers were still writing us from the Russian front, giving us hope.

But now with the Allied's air raids the war had come to our town. My school mates and I was only thirteen but we already had to do war time after-school chores - cleaning up the rubble after air raids, helping to put out fires or collecting metals for the war effort. We were kept very busy but I could not get Gunter out of my mind. Where was he? What is happening to him? And why?

At school, I had trouble with my class work. I could not stop staring at Gunter's empty desk. My home room teacher saw this. She said something like "our country may need their help elsewhere in winning the war. In any case, they will be well taken care of - stop thinking about it!"

I guess this is what she was expected to say, but I knew better. My parents had told me that Gunter's family had been taken away because some one had denounced his father for having said something bad about the Nazis and about the war. I understood - even we youngsters were told in our compulsory 'information sessions' that denouncing other people, even our parents, was our patriotic duty. My parents, of course, had warned me many times not ever to tell any one what we were talking about at home.

So, people simply stopped talking to each other for fear of being accused of something they said. Anything, even the slightest slip of the tongue could lead to disaster. As if the horrors of the air raids, the hushed-up bad news from the front, so many soldiers losing their lives in far away lands were not enough - now we could not even be at peace in our own homes, with our family and friends.

Somehow, life had to go on. Together with my friends I did what boys would do - playing 'cops and robbers', playing pranks on our neighbors, playing soccer and running races. There was even the Nazis' version of the Boy Scouts, officially not compulsory, but if you did not join, you could no longer count on admission to higher education. As the war was coming closer to us, our 'patriotic' indoctrination was becoming more and more intense. The ever present fear of getting into trouble for not doing enough kept hanging over us like a dark cloud.

I now began to understand what my parents had been telling me all along about the Nazis leading our country into ruin. But it took a few more years of growing up for me to ask myself the much bigger question: how was it possible that my country would go down the path to dictatorship, to ruthless oppression, to crass brutality, recklessly starting a war that would end in total chaos for so much of the world? How did this happen, of all places, here in Germany, a country once renowned for its great achievements in science, in culture, with its much envied institutions of higher learning?

Our beloved Germany had slid into a dictatorship, ruled unforgivingly by a band of nationalistic zealots, hell bent on imposing their contorted world view on our country, on the world. Law abiding as they were, most Germans submitted to their harsh rule especially after it had been given a semblance of legality.

How could this have happened in Germany, and why?

Eventually, after so many years of suffering and death, with so much of the world in ruins, the answers to these questions became clear.

Germany's Road to Dictatorship

Two decades earlier the First World War finally had ended, not because one side was clearly the victor but because each warring country was exhausted - too many killed senselessly, too much wealth destroyed, too many going hungry, too many nations bankrupted. And then, far from trying to heal, the Versailles peace treaty opened new wounds, with Germany carrying the brunt.

After the war had ended, it would take Germany over ten years to find a new balance in its economic and political life. Finally, for the first time in its history Germany had become a democracy. But right from the start, its 'Weimar Republic' was under attack from the extreme Left and Right, no party strong enough to garner a clear majority. In response to this reality the Weimar constitution provided that the party with the most votes (a plurality) would be entitled to form the government. This meant that coalitions with other parties were always necessary, leading to the need to compromise, which in itself is not a bad thing.

In the 1920s, in spite of their WWI post-war troubles, most Germans were getting comfortable with their new democratic government. They began to look beyond the trauma of a lost war. The economy was beginning to recover, the devastating inflation had wound down, people began to find jobs again. Things were looking up for them.

Until a wave of nationalism made Hitler their new leader.

Initially, Adolf Hitler's attempt to insert himself into the German political scene met mostly with disdain and contempt. After all, he was a total outsider, an Austrian and thus not even a German, with only rudimentary education, and certainly not a part of the ruling class. He had laid out his ideas in his book "Mein Kampf": to establish an authoritarian regime, to prepare Germany for war again, and declaring the Jews to be at the root of all problems. All this seemed so preposterous to most Germans that they were ready to dismiss him as a silly rebel-rouser. They came to regret it.

It would take Hitler twelve years of hateful oratory, an unending series of riotous rallies, and vicious street fighting by his private army, to finally garner enough votes to make his party Germany's largest - with just 30% voting for him in Germany's last free election. But under the Weimar constitution, this entitled him to form a new government which he did on January 30, 1933.

Much later, after all the damage had been done, many Germans asked themselves: How was it possible that a person like Hitler could wind up to be their leader, in a Nation so steeped in tradition and valuing education and ethics as much as it did?

It turned out that Hitler succeeded precisely because he was not "One of Theirs". Instead, he cunningly 'branded' himself as the champion of all those who had been left behind in the German post-war recovery: the middle class that had lost its economic status, the workers who had been carrying the brunt of unemployment for too long, and, last but not least, the generals whose job had become obsolete after Germany's humiliating defeat.

On his march to become Germany's dictator Hitler used the same approach that had helped several of his contemporary dictators. He saw that all of them used similar programs to gain power - creating rabid followings of the dispossessed, spread fear in the streets, intimidate judges, take control of the media, and then blame everything on some hapless minorities. Once in power they would generously hand out jobs to their followers to reward them with the possessions of those who had been 'eliminated' for having opposed them. Hitler had seen how this basic program had been successfully used by every one of his contemporary dictators and he would use it, too. Here is how he implemented it:

- Hitler was the consummate demagogue, a con-artist, a compulsive liar, and with his crudeness he was appealing to many Germans' lowest instincts. His specialty was whipping up his followers with hateful oratory. He was very, very good at it.

- With his mottos: "We will make Germany great again" and "Germany First!" he seduced many unsuspecting Germans into becoming his followers, blind to the deceit behind these slogans.

- Ignoring the legal process, Hitler immediately started to rule by executive orders, reducing Germany's legislative institutions to rubber-stamping their approval. Government officials who dared criticize him were fired, and if they persisted, locked up.

- In rapid sequence he dismantled Germany's judicial system, dismissed dissenting judges, eliminated freedom of the press, outlawed all opposing organizations and labelling them "the enemy of the people".

- In a show of strength he proceeded with tearing up international agreements that he found onerous. It endangered the country's security but It made him popular with many Germans who otherwise would have continued in opposition.

- Next, he blamed minorities, foremost the Jews, for all the Nation's problems and ruthlessly persecuted them.

- When many Germans started to object to his trampling on all they held as their moral values he would tell them: "Look, I had told you all along that I would do all this. I even wrote it in my book for all to read. You elected me anyway, so now stop complaining - or else...!"

- When this was not enough to fend off his critics he did what dictators like to do - he started a war which would divert attention away from his Nazis' outrageous behavior and it would end any remaining opposition, all in the name of patriotism.

To seize power was one thing, but how would Hitler manage to stay there? He and his cronies were very much aware that not even one third of the German electorate had voted for him. Soon after having seized power, there was growing unrest among many Germans because of the Nazis' heavy-handed behavior. Not even a year into his reign, he already felt threatened by serious opposition, especially from within his own ranks, from his very own private militia. He knew he had to do something dramatic to secure himself in his newly obtained position of power.

In a move reminiscent of Stalin's purges Hitler had the leaders of his inner opposition killed. It sent shock waves through Germany.

How was Hitler able to get away, literally, with murder? How would he get away with the many horrendous crimes that he and his henchmen would commit in the years to come? He could do it because he had 'stacked' the courts with judges from his own party who predictably did nothing to prosecute him. Also, the German press was already controlled by Hitler's Ministry of Propaganda which was spinning his purge as "the ultimate sacrifice for the good of the nation". For those who were still voicing their objection, his newly created network of concentration camps was ready. Just enough about the atrocities committed there was leaked out in carefully measured doses, enough to spread terrible fear.

But still there were enough Germans who were determined to end his reign of terror, especially those who had been close to the victims of his purges. Hitler, of course, was keenly aware that many Germans were just waiting for an opportunity to take him down - just a few years into his reign he had narrowly escaped eleven attempts on his life already. (At least one of them, the one on November 8, 1939, was most likely a staged affair. It was carefully orchestrated to have Hitler leave the scene a few minutes earlier than planned, under the pretext of 'scheduling changes' and thus he escaped the big explosion. He would use it as a welcome pretext to unleash yet another sweeping purge of Hitler's opponents, those who had tried to stop WWII. Faking assassination attempts is a favorite ploy among dictators.)

Hitler became paranoid about his own safety and responded to each of these crises with ever escalating repression and cruelties - his first foul deed, the killing of his nearest competitors for power made it necessary for him to fight for his survival with new repression, new violence, new killings of real or imagined challengers.

All dictators eventually will fall into this cycle of violence.

As a result of his paranoid fears, he and his inner circle developed a 'bunker mentality' closing themselves off, trying to shield themselves from their own people. However, in doing this they also removed themselves from the realities of the life of their Nation, causing them to make one bad decision after another.

Hitler had succeeded beyond his wildest dreams - he was the uncontested master of Germany. At this pinnacle of his career as politician you might assume that he would now settle into a new phase where he would begin to enjoy his position as the leader of a great nation, reluctantly acknowledged by the world as a reality to be reckoned with. Like all men of great power he now became totally consumed with securing his newly achieved exalted status.

He demanded every one to swear an oath of unconditional loyalty to him personally and to the Nazi flag (the Swastica). Those who would hesitate to do so would be eliminated one way or the other, from just getting fired or somehow disappearing - 'accidents happen.' This made it so much easier for him to rule the country, unchallenged from other views about what would be good for the country.

But as a result, Hitler wound up surrounded with 'yes-men', unwilling to give him contrarian advise for fear of offending his fragile ego. There was no one left in his inner circle to prevent their inexperienced "Commander-in-Chief" from committing one military blunder after another.

Then Hitler embarked on an all-out program to 'brand' himself as a leader unmatched in history, as standing above everything and everybody, and especially above the Law. The personality cult he created for himself as Germany's 'Fuehrer' was aimed at making him unassailable in the eyes of his people, which is exactly what a dictator needs as a shield against any possible future challenge to his authority. Every school room, every home, every government office was to display a portrait of Hitler. He wanted everyone to wear the insignia of the Swastica, the Nazi symbol. Not wearing one, or not having Hitler's portrait hanging in your living room would already make you suspect.

Keenly aware of the power of symbolism, Hitler made the Nazi Swastica icon appear everywhere, and displaying the newly created German Swastica flag became obligatory. Not to always display this flag automatically would mark you as an opponent, often with dire consequences. You just could not get a job unless you wore the Nazi symbol on your lapel.

Was Hitler sincere in his belief that he was the 'savior' of his country, or was he just the typical pandering politician? Did he really believe all this stuff about his great love for the German nation, and all the venom he was spouting at his adversaries? Or was he a total cynic, simply tuning out, or even enjoying the monstrous crimes committed in his name? Perhaps we will never really know.

But one thing is sure - every single step that Hitler took to eventually get complete control over his Nation could have shown the Germans where he was heading. He became their dictator not by one single dramatic move, but in relatively small increments.

The Great Lure of the 'Good Economy'

Politicians know they will not stay in office long if the economy is not good. Not even the most debased dictatorship can survive if fathers cannot provide for their families and mothers cannot feed their children.

In order to get elected every candidate will be harping on the promise of jobs and good pay. For normal politicians any promise made during the campaign can be blissfully ignored once in office. But not for the aspiring dictator - doing away with unemployment, making the economy bustling again is the key to maintain his position of power. Whatever it takes he absolutely must make sure that every one will have a job, with the best ones naturally going to his followers.

'Full employment' was a fail-safe way for Hitler to gain approval even from those who originally had opposed him. Even Germany's Socialists, originally Hitler's most outspoken opponents, came around to quietly supporting him when they saw that he indeed had done away with unemployment within just a few years after taking over.

Dictators, of course, do not do this 'full employment' bid out of compassion for the poor. They know that any one who has been saved from the hardship and the humiliation of long periods without a job will be forever a grateful follower. Few of them will ever raise the question about the methods used to create their jobs. And few of them will ever realize that they are now totally beholden to their Dictator - the specter of ever losing his job again will make almost every person submit to the most debasing action - anything not to lose the job, and he knows that if he does not play along, he may never get a job again.

Any one who just got a good job after years of unemployment is quite willing to overlook injustice and violence done to some one else, especially when he is told that this 'some one else' is one of those 'leaches to society' who the Dictator's propaganda had been painted as responsible for past unemployments.

And, most likely, in his new good job he will not really want to know about the real reason the job came into being. But look how Hitler 'created' all these new jobs - by a massive build-up of the military and the armament industries camouflaged as 'public works programs'. Nevertheless, for the 'man in the street' things looked pretty good, and soon the Germans saw this as the "Great Hitler Economy". Little did they know that the Nazis had achieved this 'miracle' by running up enormous deficits to finance their war preparation. Five years into Hitler's reign the country was essentially bankrupt.

This is when Hitler and his cronies came up with the time-honored way to shore up their dwindling treasury: they must get some one else to pay who cannot say no - hence the well-orchestrated "Kristallnacht" to frighten the German Jews into surrendering their wealth to the Reich. When even that massive robbery was not enough to righten the tattered German finances the Nazis started the war to take what they needed by brute force.

Once on this disastrous course, the Nazis found out that one foul deed would make the next one inevitable - after taking everything from their first war target (Poland) they went on to invade other countries, for new looting. Of course, there was always a totally different reason given for invading another country - it was aways the 'other' that was blamed.

It would take five years of a disastrous war that would bring an end to this cycle. This was what Germany did under Hitler's dictatorship, and predictably he had done what all dictators see as their way out of the mess they had created for their nation - do one more foul deed after another.

The edifice that Dictators build is based on deceit and recklessness. Sooner or later, the people will have to pay for it.

Life under a Dictatorship

"The best political weapon is the weapon of terror."
Heinrich Himmler, Chief of the Gestapo

It's not difficult to trace the ways by which a nation can slide into dictatorship, from the safety of distance, in time and space. The 'big picture' is easy to see, but how about all the ordinary citizens? How do they feel about what is happening to them, how do they look at their government from their own personal perspective?

Their lives must, somehow, go on, even though they are very much aware that they have lost much of their personal freedom, and that they no longer can count on a reliable system of justice. For most of them, their basic priorities have not changed - to have a family, to provide for them, to come home to them after the end of the work day, and maybe to spend some time with their friends.

But they have to be careful. They must make sure that they do nothing that would make their party block warden report them for even the most insignificant comment. They must be sure to make enough of an effort to participate in the weekly indoctrination session. They must show deference to even the most hated local party boss. They must swallow hard when they hear their teenage sons spout the worst propaganda slogans, when their daughter joins the most rabid youth group.

Everything becomes a matter of survival by conforming to whatever instructions come their way. The most successful of those who survive unharmed are those who have made themselves look as if they had fully identified with the system. Actually, they are the ones the dictator is most afraid of - it makes them suspicious of hidden thoughts. Those who have not learned to hide their own feelings will go from one scare to another but in the end, they usually are not the ones who were 'interrogated'.

The final effect is the loss of understanding of what is true and what is not, which relationship is right and which is false. Once this has become a collective loss, the dictator has won. From that point on, everything can happen, even the most outrageous travesties of justice and morality. And so it did happen, to me, and to millions of others.

What we experienced in Nazi Germany was an 'all-time high' in terror and barbarity, and an 'all-time low' in morality. None of this came to us at once, all of it was slow in coming, one act of violence and injustice at a time. Did we ever get numb to it?

It would take no time at all until our family got its first taste of the life to come under the Nazi regime. No sooner had it risen to power in 1933 the Nazi party began terrorizing all Germans with its private militia, the infamous 'Sturmabteilung' (the SA), intimidating and brutally beating anyone who dared to oppose them. This SA was a collection of rowdies and the disgruntled that seemed to hate any one who stood for law and order. The Jewish population was their preferred scapegoat for all the ills of the times, the lost war, the awful German economic depression and runaway inflation. The Nazis seemed eager for the next great war to start, which would eventually destroy Germany and condemn all of Europe to a daily fight for food and shelter in a seemingly endless struggle for survival.

Like all dictators, the Nazis just about perfected the many ways to blunt any remaining resistance to their regime. The threat of being hauled in for 'interrogation' was already bad. Everyone knew what that would mean. The fear of winding up in concentration camp was enough to bend the will of the strongest. We knew that the camps existed, and we knew that they were awful, but few knew the full extent of their horrors until after the war. Another devilishly effective way the Nazis beat people into submission was to simply withhold rationing cards. Without a ration card, it was completely impossible to live.

Then the Nazis introduced the particularly odious practice of "Sippenhaft," making your relatives legally responsible for your compliance. What a frightening thought that your father or mother or brother or sister could be hauled away for your alleged misdeeds! It was deliberately designed by the Nazis to bend even the strongest to their will. These threats to family members were in fact even more effective than the actual terror acts.

Denouncing, with truly dire consequences, happened all the time, and were another effective method of controlling the populace. Children denounced parents, businessmen denounced competitors, employees denounced rivals - treachery was everywhere. It was easy; any little whisper was enough to get you hauled in for 'interrogation', and even if you were set free, you were branded as an "enemy of the Vaterland." To get a feel for this mentality, watch "The Lives of Others," a movie set in post-war Communist East Germany. It could just as well have shown our life under the Nazi terror. No wonder we became fearful and suspicious - you couldn't trust anyone. But I, for one, was determined not to let fear circumscribe my life.

By the way, do you know how Germans would greet each other during the Nazi regime? If you guess the infamous "Heil Hitler," you are only partly right. Before saying "hello," or engaging someone in a conversation, you would furtively look back over your shoulder to see whether any one was close enough to eavesdrop on your conversation. This habit became second nature to many, and earned it the sardonic moniker, "der deutsche Gruss" (the German greeting). No joke. You simply could not trust any one, period. Children were encouraged to inform on their parents, friends were set upon friends. The effect was utterly demoralizing.

My father had been relentless in his fight for a peaceful democratic Germany. He was a patriot of the best kind, having served honorably in the 'Great War' of 1914 and had seen enough of its horrors to do everything in his power to make sure that this would never happen again. All this was against everything the Nazis wanted. No wonder he wound up one of their targets to be eliminated, but his faith in justice and honor of the German people was such that he could not conceive that the Nazis would really go after him and do him harm. He was well known as a vocal opponent of the Nazis, and of the extreme left as well, the Communists. He was the Mayor of our town and a member of the regional parliament, as a delegate of Germany's Center Party, for long the country's largest. No wonder he had to endure constant attacks from the Nazis especially as he kept telling his constituents that he saw the Nazis as a really serious threat to the Nation. With his great faith in the basic decency of the German people he could not imagine that harm would come to him.

He began to receive many threats from his Nazi opponents but dismissed them as the work of crackpots. But things got pretty bad all over Germany. Finally, my father agreed to get together with his fellow party leaders who all had been warned about the danger of getting arrested by the Nazi mob, but for what, did they ask each other? We have done nothing wrong, certainly nothing illegal! They all finally understood that their safety, and that of their families, were indeed at great risk. After some stormy arguments like: "we are not running away from them, this is preposterous, illegal, and un-German!" they saw that there was no way out. They hastily packed a few necessities, and under cover of the night went to a timber-cutters' shed deep in the Black Forest, owned by of one of the other town's mayors, abandoned for the winter season.

Here, they hoped to wait a few days, to see whether the Nazi mob would simmer down, and if not, they would make their way to Switzerland on back roads, a two day's hike from where we lived. To their shock and surprise, the next morning they found themselves surrounded by the very mob they had tried to evade. They were hauled back to town and thrown into the Offenburg jail. Now the Nazis had their 'proof' - they accused these hapless would-be escapees of treason!

It was a huge blow for my father to be incarcerated - he, who always had upheld the principles of justice and freedom! He, who had fought valiantly to defend anyone threatened by Germany's growing mob mentality. At least he was not being ill treated - the prison staff knew him, and they had not yet been been perverted into what was to come in later years. But even the Nazis could not make their trumped-up charges stick in the courts. The German justice system was still working, though not for much longer. Luckily Father was released from jail after a few agonizing weeks.

Somebody obviously had told the 'authorities' of the mayors' escape plan, and to this date the identity of the informer remains a mystery. Of the three Nazi friends who knew the plan, only one survived the war: he maintained to his death that he was not the one who had betrayed them; yes, he was at that time a Nazi, but later changed his views when he saw the horrors of their regime. Besides, he was a loyal friend, and our families were very close.

Many years later his son, without any prompting from our side, emphatically defended his father's innocence, telling us that his father, to the end, lived under the burden that his good friend, Eduard Mack, probably suspected him, no matter how much he assured him of his innocence. The plain fact is that there was a betrayal. This is just one of the innumerable personal tragedies that are born by political terror, in Germany, and anywhere in this world, wherever it is allowed to take root.

Where were all these proud burghers when the Nazi mob descended on their towns and arrested their leaders? They did what so many in Germany, and in other places on this earth do when faced by lawlessness and the threat of physical harm. They retreated into what they thought was the safety of their homes and stayed quiet, heads in the sand, trying not to attract the ire of the mob. And there were many seemingly 'good' Germans, who changed their allegiance over to the Hitler party, some because they hoped for salvation from the ills of the dismal post-war times, and some because it was the convenient thing to do. To protect their careers, their comfort, they threw in with the tide of Nazism, ignoring dire warnings from people like my father. Many found out, to their great dismay, that this would not save them anyway.

It hurt my father immensely to be abandoned by the very people he had served so loyally in the difficult times after the Great War. He had helped them through the devastating German hyperinflation, the deep depression of the later 1920's, and the rising political violence of the early thirties, only to watch too many of his townspeople join in support of the evil Nazi regime. This story repeated itself a thousand times throughout Germany, in the Nazis' exhilaration enforcing their newly found unchallenged power.

While my father was still in the Offenburg prison we were evicted from our grand Rathaus residence. Mama and her four children would have literally been out in the street, but my father's relatives intervened: they helped us move into a reasonably comfortable apartment in Karlsruhe, then the state capital, where we were ordered to stay, along with many others that were designated as "unreliable persons requiring police surveillance." Here, after my father's release a few weeks later, the family settled in for an uneasy life marked by fear of making any misstep that would give new reason for being taken in for questioning. And for the first time, our family was dreadfully poor. Above all, my father had a hard time getting over his dismissal and the injustice he and his family had been forced to endure.

Life for us youngsters became clearly divided into two very separate spheres: an orderly, pleasant life inside the family, and a turbulent one every where else. There were the rules and the moral convictions of the family, expressed in no uncertain terms by my father and the quiet determination of my mother to maintain an orderly and caring home. There were lively, often passionate discussions about the outside world, the increasing Nazi oppression of "people like us," but we were also very much aware that nothing so freely discussed inside the family could ever be repeated, or even alluded to, to any one outside.

At first, being still little children we did not understand what was going on around us. Once we were a little older we could see the relentless indoctrination efforts by the Nazi propaganda machine, force-feeding the German people an endless succession of lies. We could see, increasingly, the physical signs of the growing Nazi terror, the arrests, the beatings, the quiet disappearing of people we knew, people who dared to voice their opposition to the Nazis. Like so many other Germans, our family had to make the hard decisions either to continue to speak our rejection of Nazism, or to behave more cautiously, and then maybe survive. Even mildly criticizing the Nazis, even cracking a joke at their pompous little despots was not allowed - dictators and their underlings are very much aware that 'ridicule can kill'. Accordingly, penalties were severe. It was a constant 'tight rope' dance.

For the average German, it was getting very complicated. Should all Germans have revolted at enormous risk for their and their families' existence? Where were the institutions, the leaders, who would guide the Germans in such an effort? Easy to judge from the perspective of a free nation that had never experienced political terror of this magnitude.

We will be well advised to see to it that our democratic institutions will always remain intact to serve as guaranty for our freedoms. Any attack on them are to be resisted - now, not when it will be too late.

Family - always the Refuge?

We will never run out of bad things to say about the Nazis, but perhaps one could give them a grudging bit of credit for always being consistent and absolutely transparent about their plans. Unlike most politicians who promise one thing and then, once in power do something else, the Nazis carried out exactly what they had said they would do: they put everyone who would oppose them in jail, cruelly persecute Jews, gypsies, homosexuals, intellectuals, and anyone else they decided not to like, and then they started World War II, mainly to grab land for their so-called "Master Race." Throughout these times, average Germans found themselves wishing that the Nazis had been as dishonest about their aims as most politicians and would go back to 'business as usual' once they had succeeded in securing power.

You see, most Germans expected this to happen with the Nazis and many were sorely disappointed that the Nazis turned out to be true to their word in being every bit as evil and ruthless as they said they would be. To everybody's horror and surprise, the Nazis found seemingly limitless ways to use terror to stay in power. Much to German people's lasting disgrace, altogether too many Germans tacitly supported the Nazis' madness when there was still time to resist, fearful for their own lives and the lives of their loved ones.

Our extended family was solidly in my father's court, except for Mama's older brother Hermann. A much decorated WWI hero, he had survived a shot in his head and lost one eye. I remember him fondly for his inexhaustible supply of jokes, some not fit for polite society, which endeared him much to us youngsters. Like Father, he was in the highly regarded German Civil Service. Cutting a dashing figure as a Lieutenant in the Kaiser's Army, he moved in 'higher circles' and married a girl from the local nobility. His wife was ambitious, and following the fashionable trend, she became a rabid Nazi. Rumors had it that she had developed a rather cozy relationship with our State's notorious Governor Wagner and thereby managed to catapult her husband to become his right-hand man. In his position of power, Onkel Hermann offered to help Father re-enter his career, but only if Father would agree to become a member of the Nazi party. This, of course, he refused to do.

Though beleaguered from all sides, he would not budge. His friends would lean on him: "Come on now, don't be so stubborn. It's the new way of things, just make some allowances and swallow your pride. Get with it whether you like the bastards or not - they are the new reality!"

Mama would say: "I know you are hurting terribly. What they have done to you is awful. But we have to live, and as long as you oppose them you will not be allowed to work. Like it or not, think of your family!"

Brothers Hermann and Waldemar, then in their teens and heading for college were worried, too: "Papa, please do something. Already we are not allowed to play soccer with them. They will expel us, and then what? How can you kill our chances! We won't be able to go on to university! And why not join our German renewal? What's so difficult about being a good German?"

My sister Anneliese and I were too young then to understand all of this. We were lovingly shielded by Mama and Papa from their fears and their suffering. But nothing could keep us from listening to their arguments through closed doors.

Well, my father was stubborn. He had an unshakable faith in the basic decency of the German people and felt sure that the country would not stand for all this Nazi nonsense for long. And his final words in all these heated arguments were "if more of you would speak out against this abomination we would be able to change it." But too many Germans would not heed his words. Too many were betting on the Hitler regime being as short-lived as all the other political coalitions in the years before.

They were terribly wrong: Not only did the Nazis stay in power, but they got a lot worse. And, sure enough, when the time came for Hermann and Waldemar to apply for university, they were told not to waste their time. No way would they be admitted with an 'Un-German' father like that. The fact that by that time they had done their compulsory military service did not mean anything. But then the war would come and change everything.

In the meantime there would be the usual family visits with much good-natured bantering - but those with Onkel Hermann's family were stressful to say the least. The rare visits with them would always end up in bitter arguments, mostly about why Father would not join the Nazi party and why he would continue in his vocal criticism of the Nazi's ever tightening oppression. Often I saw Onkel Hermann's wife storming out of the room hysterically threatening to tell the police or even her 'friend' the Governor. Somehow, Onkel Hermann always succeeded in smoothing things over, at least to the extent that his wife would not denounce us as "enemies of the people." These were close calls, though. Like so many families, ours was also deeply divided, certainly with Onkel Hermann's. It took a lot of effort not to let these rifts become lethal. We had to work hard not let these disputes consume us.

After the war had ended, his wife and oldest daughter Hanna committed suicide. They had been brutally abused by a mob bent on revenge. Although never accused of any war crimes, Onkel Hermann was put into prison for having served in a high position in the Nazi administration. Through his connections with the French occupation government, my father succeeded in easing his prison conditions and he arranged an early release. When asked why he would help Onkel Hermann after he had not helped my father him in his own time of distress, he would say "just because somebody has failed me is no reason for me to fail him in his time of need."

Now that is Character. Character resists expedience. It is deeply engrained, etched into a person, the main source of the ability to maintain a person's integrity under the duress of a dictatorship. My father's strength of convictions determined my own for the rest of my life.

Our larger family, which had always been a place of peace and cooperation was being torn apart. We tried hard not to let this happen. Family is our most basic social institution and the source of our strength. Keep the family together even when the past brings a lot of heavy baggage.

40

Where do you go for Help?

Faced with the ever increasing oppression by the Nazi regime, many Germans were looking for political and emotional help from the nation's institutions and, of course, from their religion.. The first to disappoint the Germans in this search was the judiciary - the judges had sold themselves to the Nazis, just to be sure that they would keep their jobs.

Then we were looking to our military, traditionally an 'unpolitical' force claiming for themselves the highest standards of patriotism and honor. The military was dominated by the sons of the German aristocracy, who in addition to their position of power also had a high degree of financial independence - most of them came from the rich landowner families. To our terrible disappointment and to their everlasting shame these men turned out to be the worst cowards when confronted with the bullying by Hitler and the other Nazi goons.

That left the religious institutions. With very few exceptions, they, too, failed their flock. We had witnessed the Catholic Church's reprehensible complicity with the Nazis, when saving its own position became more important to them than protecting its faithful. After all, the Vatican had made an odious agreement with Hitler, the infamous 'Concordat' by which the Church consented to stay quiet in exchange for the safety of its clergy and its property. The Church found it much more important to insist on doctrine and dogma than speaking out against the actual evil in the real world. We believed there were much more pressing problems than doctrines, like why eating meat on Fridays would land us in hell (most of the time there was no meat to eat anyway).

Where can one turn for safety and consolation if not even to religious institutions, when you can not even open up to your spiritual advisor whom you are supposed to trust? It leaves you with a devastating feeling of loneliness, of hopelessness. In the end, stripped of a lot of useless trappings, our religious life became more deeply spiritual, looking to its uplifting elements, and simply living by the Golden Rule:

"Do unto others as you want them to do unto you."

The one place you could hope to find support was your immediate family. But the Nazis had succeeded in sowing mistrust even there with their constant reminder that what was discussed within the family was not safe from scrutiny either. We learned to be careful.

But the Nazis had succeeded in sowing mistrust into almost all families, and we learned to be careful and to fend for ourselves as best we could. Survival was the issue. True, too many Germans at that time made compromises that in hindsight seem dreadfully wrong. It's easy to judge them now, but you can only understand when you are in the middle of oppression and aware of the dire consequences for yourself and your wife and your children.

Especially after the war had started, we would hear more and more often about people being detained for the most trivial reasons - for cracking a joke about the lack of food, or about some Nazi official that had made a fool of himself. And then, the whispered news of someone in our neighborhood having disappeared. You had to be very careful indeed.

Yet there were enduring friendships. Our neighbor around the corner was the principal of the elementary school, a burly man who was all authority, at least in our eyes. He was a highly decorated veteran of the first world war, in which he had lost his right arm. Their two daughters were in school with my sister and me, but a bit older. Our parents knew each other also from church, and they gradually developed enough confidence in each other to talk about all kind of matters that usually are only covered among the closest of friends. Our 'Victory Garden' backed up to theirs, and eventually we would go together foraging for some extra food in the country-side. But most of the time, we cautiously kept apart, like everyone else, not willing to risk a breach of trust.

But once we were invited into their home for a birthday party!

A party! A break from the dreary everyday fight for food, the never ending air raid drills, the Nazi 'Information Meetings.' Even I, writing about this seemingly little event some seventy years later, get emotional how much such a small social gathering had meant to us. How can anyone possibly understand who has not lived through periods like these?

For us at that time, it was a wondrous break in our dark war days. We were happy with any little thing that would bring us a light moment. Perhaps there would even be a small cake, a little juice, and for our parents perhaps a cup of 'Ersatz' coffee. We knew not to expect anything more. We, like they, had little to spare, but it didn't matter. We excitedly rehearsed the little poem we wanted to recite as our birthday present.

I still remember how they had decorated their home. Flowers everywhere, the table set with their fine china, an embroidered tablecloth and matching napkins - the 'gemuetlich' German middle class setting just as it should be. We sang, we recited poems, we drank, and we ate the delicious cake. Her father broke out the brandy he had saved for this occasion. Warm happiness all around.

Then the birthday girl stood up. Glowing with pride, she announced to her parents that she had signed up to join the 'Lebensborn' to have a baby for her Fuehrer and the Vaterland.

For a moment there was stunned silence. It was as though we were frozen in our chairs. Her father glared at her trying to understand. "What did you say?" was all he could get out. Again: "What did you say?"

Not quite so sure of herself any more she said "well, now that I am eighteen, I am able to do my duty to my country."

Her father and mother looked at each other in disbelief. Then all hell broke loose. Her mother cried hysterically, her father, red in the face, thundered "how could you do such a thing - are you out of your mind?"

He could not believe it. Here stood his daughter, in his eyes still his sweet little girl, in her youthful determination to do what her group leader had put into her head: "You are to have a baby for your country from a true Arian!"

Her father would not have any of this. No way. "You go right now and tell your Leader that you are not going to do this, no way!"

Defiant, looking her father straight into the eye she yelled: "Nobody, not you, not anybody, will keep me from doing my duty! And I will tell my Leader what you said!" At that, we all fell silent. Would she really denounce her parents? So many others had done this awful thing. Even my sister and I, then only 13 and 14 years old, knew what that meant - interrogations, stern warnings at best, and most likely a lot worse. Marked an 'Enemy of the Vaterland' her father would be removed from his position, and then what?

The party was over. My father shook his friend's hand and looking into his eyes for a long moment, signaling his full support, as mother gave her sobbing friend a warm embrace. There was nothing else we could do.

In their unfathomable immorality, the Nazis had created this 'Lebensborn' in the middle of WWII in response to Germany's staggering human losses. It was an institution where soldiers meeting the Nazi criteria of the 'Master Race' would be invited to impregnate young girls. Their babies would be given up to special orphanages to be raised to become good Nazis - and cannon fodder for future wars - a flagrant case of the State imposing its morbid concept of morality on brain-washed young people who simply no longer knew better.

Fortunately, what could have been an absolute horror ended well enough. She rescinded her decision to enter the 'Lebensborn,' citing her commitment to nursing convalescent soldiers in the nearby military hospital. No doubt, her family's solid morality came through. Surely it also helped that she saw the same convictions in her neighbors. Contrary to what the rest of the world had thought at that time, not all Germans had lost their moral compass. Although the world found it hard to believe, many, many Germans held on their core beliefs in decency and personal honor, even in the face of the most ruthless oppression.

Then came the War.

It would change everything.

On the First of September 1939, without provocation, Germany invaded Poland, mainly in order to take its land for the German "Master Race". In his campaign, and even in his manifesto "Mein Kampf" Hitler had said clearly that eventually he would take Poland's land by force. Now, after seven years of reckless spending on re-arming, Germany once again was nearly bankrupt. Taking Poland with its vast land resource, he hoped, would solve Germany's food supply problem.

It was a huge miscalculation. Hitler had assumed that the Allied would not come to Poland's aid as obligated under their mutual defense treaty. Why this risky assumption? Because Hitler had seen that in every one of his previous aggressions the Allied had not done anything to stop him. Here is what led Hitler to make his mistake:

Two years into his reign many Germans were getting impatient with Hitler. In spite of all the high-flying promises, living under his regime was not getting much better. Re-armament absorbed just about all of

Germany's resources, and as a result food was scarce and expensive. There was a constant call for more and more compulsory services which left little time for family and friends. Hitler knew he had to do something to get his people to rally behind him again.

So, In March of 1936 Hitler ordered his army to throw out the French from the formerly German provinces west of the Rhine river. The French had occupied them ever since the end of the First World War. Hitler could count on the Germans to follow him enthusiastically into this venture because it certainly would be seen as the patriotic thing to do.

The French decided not to fight. They did not want to precipitate yet another war. Against everyone's expectations, the rest of the Allied also did nothing, even though by their post-WWI agreements they were obliged to step in to help the French.

Now Hitler had finally become popular with just about all Germans. He had shown that Germany indeed was getting the world's respect again. Nobody seemed to think about how close his aggression had actually gotten to yet another European war.

Then, three years later, Hitler decided to annex Czechoslovakia. This time it was not so much for making the Germans more proud - it was to gain access to that country's armament industries and, of course, to its gold. Again, the Allied did nothing to defend their Czech allies.

So, Hitler concluded when he would take Poland, the Allied would again do nothing. But this time they did. They declared war on Germany and thus the Second World War got on its way.

Hitler and his cabal were dumbfounded. True, conquering Poland had given them what they were after - immediate access to Poland's treasury and its ample supply of food and workers. Having been taken by surprise, defeating the Polish army had been easy, but Germany at that time was still woefully unprepared for a war with the combined forces of France and England. So, for the next seven months, nothing war-like was happening.

This was the time when Germany - and the Allied - could have easily stopped the war from getting out of hand but Hitler, the dictator, could not think about anything but raw power. Moreover, the war had now given the Nazis justification to crush the internal opposition which had been growing in response to the Nazis' ever more oppressive dictatorship. Just like warmongers anywhere, they sold their war to the Germans as a somehow noble cause forced upon them by our evil neighbors.

As always, it would be the fathers, the mothers and the children everywhere who would carry the awful burdens of war. As it turned out, our family would have to shoulder more than our fair share of it.

Let's start with stories about my brothers. Hermann, twelve years older, had not liked the military, and certainly had no desire to be in the war - it prevented him from going on to university and living the life he wanted. He had learned from Father how despicable the Nazis were, but the truth is that Hermann was not entirely immune to the trappings of his rising position in the army. He cherished riding next to the commander at the head of his unit of foot soldiers (yes, until the middle of the World War, German army officers still were riding on horse back in front of their soldiers!) In the summer of 1942 his unit headed to the Eastern front, the prospect of which struck fear into the hardest heart.

But we were hopeful - just weeks before, he had been assigned to divisional headquarters to serve as deployment officer. The higher-ups had seen that he was an excellent planner. We thought this might keep him from the worst of the fighting, in their advance to what we only learned later would be the battle of Stalingrad. Our hopes were dashed cruelly later that summer when we learned that had been "killed in action".

Terribly frightened, Anneliese and I clung to each other, while Mama sobbed uncontrollably, and Father screamed out his pain. His oldest son, with so much promise, was now dead because an irresponsible madman had plunged Germany into an absolutely insane war. Father had been seething with disgust inside all along at the Nazis' deceits and ruthlessness, but now he was all fury, and he wasn't careful about who knew it. His open show of hatred of the Nazi regime would have been enough to land him in a concentration camp had it not been for the local Nazi administrators who, for once, showed forbearance out of respect for our loss. In some of them, at least, their humanity was not entirely lost yet.

I was twelve at that time, and was too stunned to know how to deal with the loss of my brother. Hermann was twenty-four at his death, double my age then. He was the quintessential older brother, who I looked up to as my role model, my confidant, and as a source of pride when he would come home on leave and I could show him off to my schoolmates. He was strong in every sense, serious in everything he did, in school, in sports, in his friendships. Much to my regret, he never bragged about any of his exploits in athletics, especially in swimming - he was the one who taught me. He also was an excellent horseman. I still have a trophy of one of his jumping competitions. And he wouldn't talk about his experiences as a soldier. But his quiet self-assurance left no doubt about his leadership qualities. You could see that he would have a great future, one day with a fine family and an enviable career. Now all that was lost forever.

Brother Waldemar was different. He was older than me by ten years, but was much more of a buddy to me. He was lots of fun to be with, irreverent and ready to laugh and joke in every situation. His astute mind readily saw through the lies and hypocrisies of the Nazis. He was a master at poking not so gentle fun at everybody and everything. Anneliese and I loved him for his quick wit, but Father, much more serious in nature, did not appreciate it at all. He would often scold him for not doing better at school and became furious with him every time he would receive a reprimand from his teachers for 'lack of respect' and 'challenging their authority.' But that is what I loved most about him.

As you would expect, Waldemar truly hated being a soldier, and made no bones about it. Not surprisingly, this got him into trouble in the military. What saved him in these (potentially serious) confrontations was his uncanny ability to see through seemingly complex logistics situations, even under the stress of combat. This made him valuable in the eyes of his commanders, and saved him in his run-ins with the military hierarchy. He would become an expert in field communications, and this probably kept him alive for three horrible years on the eastern front. Wounded several times, we would see him on his hard-earned furloughs during his recuperations. He had never been physically very strong, and we were amazed that he could handle so much pain and misery. It was clear to see that he was being worn down by a war that he hated with every fiber of his being.

I will never forget when he came down the street on his last unannounced furlough. We were walking back home from church, and he appeared a few blocks up the street, limping slowly, leaning heavily on a cane, his uniform hanging loosely on his emaciated frame. I saw him first and cried out, "Here is Waldemar, Waldemar is here!" It took a few moments for his own parents to recognize their son. Their boy, so full of joy for life before, now was a broken shell of his former self. To see him sent back to the front soon afterward was an unbearable heartbreak for us all.

A few weeks later, he wrote to us that he was not to go back to the eastern front. His leg injuries were bad enough that he could no longer walk without a cane. In carefully chosen words that only we would be able to understand he let us know that he was now stationed 'near our old home across the river.' That could only mean in nearby France, in Alsace. We were ecstatic at this news. In our wishful thinking, this meant that he would be safe, far away from the hellish eastern front.

That was the last we heard from him. In the chaos of the last months of the war, all communications broke down. There was no notification of his death at all. Not from the military, not from the Red Cross, not from any possible source, not even that he was 'missing.' Just silence. When Hermann's death had been announced to us we were stunned, anguished, and furious, but there was some level of sanity to be found in its clear finality. In the total void of information about Waldemar's fate, our family sank into a state of quiet despair. Like most Germans at that point, we were worn out from over four years of war. So much death, so much misery, so much meaningless destruction. The uncertainty about Waldemar gnawed at us constantly.

We would not learn about his death until years later, buried in the Niederbronn war cemetery, in nearby Alsace.

A few years later, Anneliese and I took Mama there. Even then, her grief was almost unbearable for us to witness. I will never forget her saying over and over, looking at the thousands of grave markers:

> *"Every one of these men had mothers and fathers.*
> *They may have come from different walks of life,*
> *but all of them had one thing in common -*
> *not one of them wanted to end up here."*

And then the War came to me.

At fourteen, all boys were inducted into the "Hitler-Youth," the obligatory paramilitary Nazi youth organization. Before any Nazi brainwashing could take root in me the war came closer, and we were ordered to spend our time cleaning up after air raids and helping to manage the increasing flood of refugees. Then, at the end of September 1944, we were marched off with thousands of other youngsters and old people, men and women, and told to dig defense trenches. My group was sent to the university city of Freiburg, a two days trek on foot.

We started with the traditional zig-zag infantry trenches on Freiburg's mountainside vineyards, famed for their light Burgundy-style red wines. We were working the hills with pick-ax and shovels, ten hours a day, sleeping in barns on hay, with cows and horses. It very soon stopped being fun. My buddy Rudi Berger, always cheerful, kept cracking silly jokes to keep us entertained. It did help a little but we were always cold, wet and hungry. The local vintners hated us for destroying their old vineyards, which had been their livelihood for generations.

Things got worse. At the end of October we were ordered to start work on an anti-tank ditch. It would go straight for five miles across a valley, 10 feet deep and 15 feet wide on the top, between the steep hillsides of Freiburg's Black Forest foothills. The ditch was meant to create a barrier against the advancing Allied tanks. Imagine the sheer enormousness of the task, digging this massive trench, all by hand, with only shovels and pickaxes. It was incredibly hard work, knee-deep in mud in the cold Autumn rain. At least the rain mostly kept the Allied fighter planes from strafing us. The ruler-straight trench provided no place to take cover. On clear days, they strafed us with abandon. The killing of our fellow diggers, and the horrifying screaming of the wounded showed us what war was all about.

I was about to turn 15 and got permission to go home for a few days for a birthday celebration with my family. On November 27, the evening before my birthday, I was shouldering my backpack to start on my five mile walk to the Freiburg rail station for the trip home. Half way there, the air raid sirens started to blare. Scrambling for cover I found a nearby ditch and hunkered down to what I thought would be just another strafing. In horror, over the next few hours, I saw the entire city of Freiburg obliterated by relentless fire bombing. When most of the city had gone up in in flames, another wave of the dreaded B-17s dropped explosives to finish the job.

Needless to say, I never made it to my birthday party. In fact, I could not even tell my parents what happened, even that I was still alive - telephones lines were down and the mail would take weeks to get through. They would be frantic - all they knew was the the city of Freiburg had been totally destroyed and that I had been there.

The city burned for days, thousands died, untold others were horribly burnt. There was not enough water to douse the flames. Half of all the buildings in the city were totally destroyed, much of the rest suffered enough damage to make them uninhabitable.

As the fires burned themselves out we were ordered to enter the city to help clear the rubble and to collect the dead for burial. Many of the dead could not be identified, burnt beyond recognition, many were missing and would never be found. For them, funeral services would be held right on the ruins of their homes. There is no way to describe the horror and revulsion of this sordid task. After a few days of working in this inferno most of us youngsters were so sick and exhausted that we were sent home, never to be the same again.

In the center of Freiburg only its magnificent cathedral remained standing, not a miracle of divine intervention nor of pin-point bombing as some would come to believe, but just because it would not burn, built entirely of stone, six hundred years earlier. No one had expected that Freiburg would become a target for destruction. As a university town with world renowned hospitals, and no industry, it had no air defense capabilities. Much later, when the Allied air campaign records were opened up, it showed that "the city of Freiburg was targeted because we had pretty much run out of other sizable towns to destroy".

I had seen a lot more than anyone ever should - the horror of war is still with me. For years, I could not even stand fireworks. Most war movies still make me sick, except the very few which tell it as it really is. I like Remarque's "All Quiet on the Western Front," "Path to Glory," or "A Very Long Engagement." Glorifying anything about war is a crime against all those who have not experienced the awful reality of humans slaughtering one another.

You don't want to forget, and you do become determined to do everything possible to stay out of wars. Unfortunately, even the most democratically governed nations have not been able to do this, sometimes because there is aggression from the outside, but just as often because there are politicians whose longing for glory are too big for their conscience.

My own Legacies of War

Traumatic events are a part of every one's life. Some you can deal with and overcome, some not so well. In the best of cases you just live with your memories as best as you can. Some become neurotics, some would try to drown them out with drinking or drugs. No matter how hard you may try you can't just will them away. But you can make a conscious effort not to wallow in your past miseries. This is what everybody around me, my parents, my friends, the entire community would tell me over and over gain. No wallowing. And it worked.

But some things did stay with me. One is my claustrophobia, undoubtedly the result of so many nights in stifling air raid shelters, in deep darkness, with the ever-present fear of possibly getting buried alive. Does anyone now have any idea what it is to be thrown into total darkness, night after night? Almost all of us are now perpetually surrounded by light, even at night, with our streets lit and our night lights in our bedrooms.

We youngsters were ordered to help with patrolling the street at night. With the total black-out the nights were pitch-black. So that we would not bump into each other we were obligated to wear two-inch-size badges made of translucent radioactive materials glowing faintly, just enough to help us make out the presence of other persons. We boys were warned never to put these radioactive badges into our pants pockets........ No matter what, we would be so happy for the opportunity to be out of the bomb shelters. We would marvel at the night skies lit up by the 'Christmas trees', the flares used by the lead bomber plane to locate their targets, followed by the fireworks of explosions, tracer flak and finally the targets in flame - as long as it was at a 'safe' distance. We, of course, thought ourselves indestructible. But then it happened.

On home leave for a few days after the horrors of the Freiburg fire bombing I ignored the air raid alarm, as usual. This time I was not lucky. Some stray bombs came down too close, blowing out windows and taking off parts of our roof. You have never seen anyone racing down three flights of stairs so fast trying to make it into the hated shelter.

Something had hit the side of my head like a blow of a fist. It did not really hurt but I felt a warm stream flowing down my neck over my sweater and down my pants. In the dim light of the shelter I must have looked awful - there was blood all over me. Mama screamed in anguish imagining the worst. Actually the cut in my scalp was very small but even the smallest head wounds happen to bleed a lot. Once they had overcome their shock they laid down the law - no more playing the hero!

That night was horrible. For more than an hour our basement shelter was shaken by near-explosions. The one light bulb started flickering, then total darkness. Scared out of our wits many started to pray. Even our Nazi block warden prayed.

Emerging from our shelter, we were dazed - many homes in ruins, ours still standing but without windows and roof.

With my head bandaged much too much for my little scrape, I began to feel like a 'wounded veteran.' Unfortunately, there was no time to go around showing off to my friends. Our home no longer livable, we and our neighbors were loaded on an open truck and driven away, nobody telling us to where. Arriving at the small farm town of Achdorf, just a few miles from the Swiss border, where we were to live in some tiny rooms above the farm stables. Even the farmers had little food to spare. As fast as they could produce it, it would be confiscated for general distribution, with the army and the Nazis getting most.

To retrieve some food left in the basement of our half-destroyed home, about 15 miles away, I was sent back on my sister Anneliese's bicycle with baskets and bags, my own bike too worn and rickety. It had to be done at night because by then the Allied controlled the air space so completely that moving around at daytime you would almost certainly been strafed. The pitch dark narrow country road was total chaos, full of refugees from the advancing Allied armies, with carts pulled by horses, cows and people, all competing for space in the darkness of the winter night, desperately trying to get away, just away. I made it through to our ruined home, scooping up what I could find by groping my way in the total darkness of our basement, no lights allowed, ever. I also knew to have my ID handy because if suspected of looting I would be shot on the spot. It was a bitter cold night and somehow I made it back, received with joy, all of us ready to devour what I brought - but to our bitter disappointment most was spoiled, frozen, and the glass jars with preserves broken. Bitter indeed. But it drove home what it meant to deal with real hunger and no more hope to get anything to eat.

Together with my friend Rudi I was told to bury some horses killed in recent air raid. While digging a few yards away from me, he hit an unexploded shell. He was blown to pieces right in front of me. It became my task to run to town to tell his parents. Yes, I was crying all the way. His mother was sobbing uncontrollably, his father screaming at me: "Why did you not pick him up?" as if I could have done anything about putting him back together again. It could have been me.

By then everybody knew that the war was lost and yet the Nazi fanatics forced the continuation of their lost cause with ridiculously insufficient means: no fuel for the few cars and trucks left, almost no ammunition, no medication for the wounded, no food, nothing.

The advancing Allied kept pounding the retreating German troops and fleeing civilians who could not move away fast enough, creating havoc, leaving no escape. Switzerland, a much hoped-for refuge was literally just a couple of miles away but the Swiss had, of course, closed their border. Surrender was dangerous because you would be shot from behind, or hung if caught, mainly by the SS and other incurable Nazis. They were the only ones who had an interest in prolonging the war – before their day of reckoning would come. Can you imagine the horror when I saw for the first time a man hung from a tree? There would be more in the frenzy of the last days of the war.

Why did we all not rebel against this senseless barbarity? It was because the Nazi dictatorship had made everything that did not serve their purposes into a crime against the State and punishable by immediate execution, always done in the most cruel way. Fear had paralyzed us all, fear of the Nazi thugs, fear of the relentless attacks from the air, fear about where our next meal would come from.

How did the Nazis manage to create so much fear? Where did the Nazis find so many Germans to do their dirty work, right up to the very end?

The power of absolute dictatorship is immense, and once established, impossible to shake. Only a final catastrophe would put an end to it.

What helped the Nazis to prolong this insane war was the Allied's demand for 'unconditional surrender.' This was cruelly exploited by the Nazi propaganda machine "Now you see, our enemies are hell bent on destroying Germany, killing all of us, ravaging our women - just see how they bomb our cities!" And on and on. The Allied's insistence on "unconditional surrender" came at a time when just about all Germans were ready to give up fighting but it gave the Nazis all the justification for forbidding any type of surrender, hanging without trial anyone they suspected of 'treason'. Of course, being driven into the corners from where there would be no escape made quite a few German soldiers fight on, even when they wished they could somehow get away.

It was in these chaotic last days of the war when I received the dreaded draft notice, promptly after turning fifteen, to join the "Volkssturm". The Home Guard was the Nazis' last ditch attempt to replenish the depleted ranks of the German fighting forces. Even after just about everything else had broken down, the German drafting offices were still functioning with notorious efficiency. So, in the last senseless few months of the war's insanity I became a member of Germany's fighting forces, pitifully made up of boys and old men, armed with vintage rifles, and in tattered uniforms.

The Volkssturm was meant to stay in our home towns and to defend them once the Allied forces would attack. In the meantime we were to help in rescue efforts after air raids, putting out fires, and patrolling streets during air raids to make sure everybody was in shelters. Overwhelmed, frightened and mostly hungry, we were a sorry lot.

Occasionally, we were guarding Allied POWs until they were taken away to camps. We were under strict orders not to bother them in any form. The plain fact was that we were afraid of them, even though we had guns and they did not.

Years later I heard that many Allied POWs would complain bitterly of their treatment by their German captors and especially that they had been humiliated by being transported in freight cars. Often they would refer to them as "cattle cars". Of course, there was no insult intended - that was all that was left of the once famed German rail service! In the last years of the war it was quite normal for all of us Germans to ride in those "cattle cars." We were glad to have transportation at all.

In mid April of 1945 the French army was about to overrun our home-based defense lines. We were ordered to fall back with the retreating German forces into what we knew would become a total disaster. I was spared the final slaughter. The locals came to my parents saying "you already have lost two of your sons, let's not lose yet another one to this wretched war!" With that they hid me and a few other of the town's boys in a narrow gorge, brought some food and blankets, all at the risk of getting hanged if caught by Nazi zealots who were prowling for hapless deserters.

It was late April and the nights were still cold. Sleeping on the rain-soaked ground I never shivered as much in my life. After two days and nights in this dark damp cave-like rock formation, with sporadic gunfighting around us, the townspeople came to tell us that the Allied had taken the town. The next question was how to avoid becoming a POW. We shed our pitiful uniforms, threw away our vintage rifles and slipped away in farmers' clothes, carrying rakes and scythes. Somehow we made it home, whatever and wherever that was.

And where were all these Nazis that had told us to be brave and to sacrifice ourselves for their version of the Vaterland? They all had somehow disappeared into the miserable masses who were fleeing from the disaster that they had created out of their hateful arrogance and their immorality. They were finally unmasked as what they really were - the most detestable hypocrites and cowards, ever, melting down to nothing the moment their Leader they had so adored had abandoned them - and their country. That much for the dictator's henchmen - when the chips are down, they are nowhere to be found.

We saw the ultimate proof of what dictators and their cronies are all about - they are cowards who hide their insecurities and their own fears behind their cruelty and their bullying.

The War had ended - but not our Troubles

Growing up in times of great upheavals, deprivation and deep social changes has its benefits which, of course, are not at all visible while trudging through the misery. But a lot of learning was happening. I sometimes wonder how people go through life without ever having experienced much of its ups and downs. How can they see the whole complexity, fragility and the meaning of their lives?

No matter what was one's political orientation, losing the war was a terrible blow to every German's mind, seeing Germany so utterly destroyed and disgraced for all the horrors that it had inflicted on so many. We had known all along that the day of reckoning would be coming and that we Germans would pay a huge price. It could be no surprise to the Germans that their victors would extract more than their 'pound of flesh' from Germany and the German people. Yes, the Allied victors had come to Europe as liberators, but that would not apply to Germany - they made it plenty clear that they were here to rule with an iron fist.

Life under Allied occupation was a bitter and traumatic experience, even after the original widespread rapes and looting had stopped. Whatever factories were still operating would be dismantled for 'Reparations' to compensate all the countries conquered by Germany during the war for the destructions and their suffering.

There was strict military rule, with early evening curfew. I spent several nights in the local military jail because sometimes we would be late coming back from school, and sometimes we simply dallied a bit to bait the military police. You could not leave town without a specific permit. The Allied occupation forces were much afraid that there would be some form of continued resistance by some die-hard Nazis after the war was officially over, but with very rare exception, no such insurgency happened. The Germans truly had enough, and also because Germans were brought up to accept the big decisions imposed upon them. Nevertheless, there was much fear on all sides. In some places, revenge killings took place. But at least we could now rely again on a well functioning legal system, free from the demoralizing fears of the Nazi terror.

Germany's cities and its infrastructure were totally destroyed, and so was the Germans' spirit. It took true patriotism to get people out of their state of despair. Father was one of those fearless leaders who was ready to squarely face up to the necessity to deal with Germany's dire circumstances.

When my father was asked to resume his former position as the town's mayor he issued a 'Proclamation' to the townspeople to help them make some sense of all the calamities of the war, the devastating defeat and the daily misery they had to face. His thoughtful speech was meant to show a way forward for a dejected people and would be printed and read all over Germany:

To the People of our Town: In a time of unparalleled upheaval, I am resuming my office as your mayor. After a cataclysmic war we are facing a vast field of destruction that humanity has never seen before: destruction of our work place, our homes, and desolation of our families and the heart and soul of us Germans. Unimaginable suffering and despair has been visited upon us, and by us. We must face clearly and without any embellishment of the facts that we have lost the war and must accept responsibility for all its consequences. We have to do this without illusions. What are we to do?

First and above all, we must keep calm, and keep order. We have no choice but to follow the directives of the (Allied) Military Government without resistance and reservation. However, we should do this with clarity of mind, openness, decency and dignity. Before us is a long and rocky road to rebuild our town and country, and in spite of all thorny issues we must proceed with courage, patience and in the confidence in our basic values. We all must share in the common struggle to overcome deprivation that is hurting all of us, by sustained unselfish cooperation. Each one of us must realize that only by working together we can help ourselves. We must stay clear of disturbances and of any action that would hurt any one of us or our community.

Reconstruction of our homes and towns must be accompanied by a profound spiritual renewal and healing of all our people, above all of our young ones. They in particular have to turn away from their previous teachings and from one-sided emphasis of the physical. A deep religious responsibility before God and to our neighbors will help to bind our people together again. Only by returning to our traditional customs and morality can we hope to regain, over time, an honorable place in the Community of Nations.

We have a special love and hope for our home town. Let all of us recognize what is needed to heal the spiritual and bodily wounds of our communities. Let us do the hard work together. For this, I am asking for your cooperation.

June 22, 1945, Eduard Mack, Mayor

So it was left to those Germans who were the real patriots to deal with the mess that the Nazis had wrought. It was an almost impossible task under the harsh military occupation by the French. Under my father's direction, these patriotic Germans tried very hard to get the best possible deals for the people of our town by defusing some of the most onerous demands by the French. My father spoke some French, but for good measure he enlisted my help in translating the endless negotiation to get the French to relent (I was quite fluent in French already then). It was good teaching for me, learning something about the difficulties of re-establishing some level of understanding between the victors and us, the defeated. The more we negotiated the more we realized the depth of hatred and mistrust that Nazi Germany had inflicted on the world, and on ourselves.

Then we had to make our German compatriots understand that not complying with the dictates of the military government would lead to even harsher measures. Predictable, we would be criticized by all sides: The French would berate us and threaten us with imprisonment when we protested their vengeful taking the best homes, throwing the owners out in the street and confiscating their valuables, or when we were dragging our feet on their much hated demands for dismantling of what was left of our factories.

Predictably and unfairly he would be criticized by all sides. Some Germans would say that he did not do enough to help them against the French, not wanting to understand that in truth we had done much more than any one else to fight their edicts. To our chagrin, we found ourselves caught too often in the middle, and we as a family felt the resentment from both the French and our own people. It was a delicate balancing act and a thankless task.

Governing, even more than management, is a complicated job, whether big or small. You cannot do right by everyone all the time. In the short term, cunning may help, but principled pursuit of what's possible is more durable. And before passing judgement, as the the old Indian saying goes,"Always make yourself walk in the other guy's moccasins."

Beyond our local concern to hold our community together, there was the much bigger task to get neighboring countries to work together again. Well remembered are the great post-war European leaders who worked hard to put order back into the lives of the nations that had been hell bent on destroying each other for so long. They were remembered in history as the right leaders at the right time - Adenauer in Germany, Monet and Schumann in France, and, of course, Marshall in America. If anything good had come out from the world's painful experiences with WWII it was this new recognition that the nations of this world must sweep aside their own small differences and disputes and unite against any possible relapse into authoritarian styles of governing.

But we should never forget the thousands of local leaders that shouldered the often thankless task of picking up the pieces left by the Nazis and their war, who worked so hard to get people and neighbors back together, to learn again how to live in peace with each other. They were the real patriots.

My father was one of them. He taught me what is expected from a citizen - above all, to resist any attempt by politicians to rule without the restraints of legitimate democratic institutions. All of us must jealously guard the independence of the judiciary and the freedom of expression on all levels of private and public life. They are essential for a civilized society.

How many more dictatorships does our world have to endure to finally wake up? What will it take to make the Nations of this Earth leery of demagogues - they all are potential dictators. We must learn how to stop them early in their insidious ways to take away our freedoms for their own selfish aims. And always remember that they usually do it in small steps. Dictatorship comes to you in small increments, often imperceptibly. But the tell-tale signs are there - take notice when you see politicians 'stack' their courts, and when they bear down on the free flow of information, on the press. The time to stop a slide into dictatorship is in these early stages.

Your and your country's life depend on it.

Two

How do Nations slide into Dictatorships?

"You became guilty once you started to replace judges with those beholden to your Leader."
(Norman Birkett, Judge at the 1945 Nuremberg War Criminal Trials, addressing the defendant Hans Frank, former German Minister of Justice)

How do Politicians become Dictators?

For sixteen of my growing-up years I have lived under the Hitler dictatorship, five of these years during the horrors of the Second World War, and then another three years under the harsh military rule of the Allied occupation forces. Naturally, this is what shaped my views on the political life of nations, and especially what dictatorships do to people.

After my engineering studies in Germany, I came to the States under a Fulbright scholarship to learn about the "American Way" managing engineering teams.. Later on my work with an international corporation included assignments in Europe, South America and the Far East, after which I settled in America, raised a family and soon became integrated in many aspects of academic as well as political life. I very much appreciated the incredible opportunities that America's free society afforded me. I hope that in my very long life I have made contributions of my own to my new home country.

With my first-hand experience of the disastrous outcome of Germany's dictatorship it is not surprising that I would watch with keen interest what happened during my life time in other countries that succumbed to dictatorships of their own. Of course, the threat of communist Russia under Stalin's ruthless rule was hanging over the world like a dark cloud and influenced just about every aspect of national life everywhere. But there were also dictators popping up during the cold war in many smaller countries whether initiated by Russia or not.

How do dictatorships happen? Most of us think of a sudden military-style coup, with some rebellious generals plotting behind the gates of their military barracks to take over by sheer force of arms, sending their soldiers to storm government buildings, with guns ablaze. This is how dictatorships happen in unstable societies, in failed nations, typically in response to long periods of predatory governments. This was the setting of the 1917 Russian revolution, and Mao Zedong's "March on Beijing", and, on smaller scale, what General Stroessner did in Paraguay, Pinochet in Chile and Castro in Cuba. They all took advantage of some prolonged crises that had made their country fall into disarray, entering the political scene of their countries violently and with a lot of drama.

But in countries with basically well-established civic and political institutions dictatorships do not happen that way. There, dictatorships come about in increments, in small steps which at the time they happen are often not even given much attention by the people, until one day they wake up and find that they had lost their freedoms, their protection under the Law, and if they chose to resist, even their lives. All this can happens at the hands of legitimately chosen national leaders who somehow evolve into dictators. What are the methods they use to overcome the legal and political obstacles designed to prevent such power take-overs? Why do they inevitably wind up to become vicious in oppressing their people? And how do the people in such countries deal with having to live under a dictator's oppression and how do they eventually acquiesce?

The example of Hitler shows how he had skillfully maneuvered around the restrictions put in his way by the German political and legal system of his days. Were his methods unique, or did aspiring dictators in other countries use more or less the same script? What are a country's conditions that make it ripe for dictatorship? Is every country different or can we see a pattern, some common threads, some kind of formula that politicians can use to get a country under their personal control?

One thing we can see quite clearly is that in modern countries dictatorships do not happen by some kind of political convulsion, some kind of violent military-style take-over. *They happen in incremental steps, and by stealth.*

I chose to take a closer look at four of the 20th century dictators to illustrate these similarities becausel had first-hand experience with them - Salazar in Portugal, Franco in Spain, Peron in Argentina and Mussolini in Italy. I lived and worked in Portugal and in Spain for some time and I did business in Argentina, during their years of dictatorship. I worked in Italy years after the war when the Italians tried to pick up after the mess that Mussolini had made of their country.

I became especially familiar with the conditions that people in Portugal and in Spain had to deal with in their every day lives under their dictatorships. As a young engineer I was delegated to guide Portuguese and Spanish government-sponsored programs to replace the old uneconomical single-use wooden shipping crates with re-usable plastics ones for their most important exports - fresh fruit and vegetables. In the nineteen sixties these export products were the life blood of their struggling economies. (In their agricultural areas there was no adequate supply of suitable wood for the ever increasing demand for shipping crates, and too much of the fruits and vegetables shipped in wooden crates would spoil on the long way to the North European markets.)

Obviously, this assignment put me right into the middle of the delicate relationships between private organizations and the all-powerful government agencies. It showed me how difficult (and how dangerous) it was for the people I worked with to cope with all the uncertainties under their country's dictatorship.

Finding out more about the historic, big-picture aspects of these dictatorships is one thing. But I was most interested in hearing directly from the people I worked with. I wanted to know how it affected their personal lives, and how each one of them had to find a way to survive while trying to maintaining their personal integrity. Every little slip-up, every wrong word could land them in terrible troubles. Talking to me, a foreigner who they thought they could trust, they felt safe to open up. How could I ever forget how anxious they were to share their plight, but also how frightened they were that somehow it could get them in trouble. Needless to say, they had to be careful in all these conversations: "Big Brother is watching you!" But I remember very well what my Portuguese and my Spanish business associates thought about their national leader.

It was surprising to learn from these conversations that each one of their dictators started out quite normally as a part of his country's established political system. None of their dictators originally were rabble-rousers, each of them was well educated and to varying degrees actually enjoyed a privileged upbringing. None of them set out in life planning to become a dictator, but all of them had at least one thing in common - an outsized ego.

In every case, what triggered their ascent into dictatorship was some kind of political or economic crisis, even a relatively minor one, to which they would respond with a *messianic belief*, a deep seated conviction, that they alone knew what was ailing their nation, and that they alone knew how to fix it. It was this type of epiphany that would turn each one of them from an ordinary politician into an aspiring dictator. It is this messianic belief that is at the root of all the pains that a dictator is able to inflict on his people. It is the basis upon which a prospective dictator will sweep aside any scruples, any respect for his nation's institutions, and even its laws.

Still, even this all-consuming messianic belief is not enough to launch a politician on his path to domination. He needs to develop a large enough group of followers, fanatics who accept their leader's beliefs unquestionably. In order to get them to become dedicated followers he has to find a way to 'transfer' his messianic belief to them. The way to do this is through good old-fashioned demagoguery.

Once in power the aspiring dictator will do everything he can, legally or not, to stay there. He will 'stack' the courts with judges beholden to him, so that when he commits a crime, he will not be prosecuted. He will become overly sensitive to criticism and therefore will outlaw the free press. The more of this he does the more enemies he will make, and will become paranoid, feeling the need to get them out of his way. At one point, in doing so, he will resort to violence and commit a crime. Once he has crossed that line, this first foul deed will need to be followed up by another one, and there will be no end to this cycle - until the final day of reckoning.

What could have been done to stop their countries' decent into dictatorships? Just about every one I questioned on this matter said that they simply had not paid enough attention to the first 'tell-tale' signs that could have told them early on where their leaders were heading. In this sense, they all felt somehow responsible for having let their country's politicians get too much power. Once they saw how much of their freedom had been lost, it was too late .

Of course, every country has its own unique set of circumstance, and each of their leaders brought his own particular characteristics into their lives. My own experiences with Germany's dictatorship, and having worked in these four other dictatorship countries gave me a good understanding what methods each one of these dictators used to achieve domination of his country and how people had succumbed to their dictators. Studying these examples may be useful when we are contemplating whether, and how, future dictatorships could happen to other countries - *including our own*.

Portugal's Salazar

Antonio Salazar is the least known of these dictators but perhaps the most insidious one. After a distinguished career as economist he was elected to Portugal's Parliament and named Prime Minister in 1932. He would rule his country for 36 years with "iron fists in velvet gloves". At the time he became the head of government, Portugal was just getting out from under a severe economic depression, with rich landowners pitted against their impoverished peasants, wealthy merchants against their servant class. Under the motto "only unity can save our country" Salazar cunningly extracted one concession after another from his legislature until he was de facto Portugal's sole ruler.

His slogans were very effective. Who could find fault with his call for "unity"? To appeal to those who were demanding meaningful reforms he found another slogan, "The New State".

But with these unrelenting battle cries he eliminated workers unions, dismissed independent thinking judges and government officials, and forcing the press to publish only his editorials, making it in effect into his propaganda machine. Whoever did not abide would be sent to prisons, often in Portugal's African colonies, or simply disappear. When oppression was no longer enough to keep him safely in power he started a war, ostensibly to revive Portugal's ancient colonial empire. With this cunning stroke he succeeded in keeping his growing opposition at bay and at the same time appealed to the masses with his fantasy of making Portugal a world power again.

So, what have we seen here? Salazar used four time-honored methods to gain, and to keep, his dictatorial powers:

- First, he selected the groups of dispossessed from each sector of Portugal's society as his standard bearers, eventually becoming his private police to enforce his edicts,

- Then he made the judiciary compliant by stacking the courts with his supporters. When he made his goons kill opposition leaders no court would prosecute him,

- Then he made the press do his bidding by forcing them to regularly publish his own editorials - a very shrewd move, avoiding out-lawing the press.

- By masterful these deceptions and using his own secret police he was able to hang on to his role as sole leader for almost thirty six years. In the end, when everything was failing around him, he started his Angola colonial war, putting an end to all remaining opposition.

But why, when he had already achieved such control over his country, did he resort to cruelly punish any one who dared to oppose his measures? It was precisely because he was so convinced of the righteousness of his beliefs that he simply no longer had any tolerance for dissent of any type. As he resorted to more and more violence to enforce his edicts he began to see more and more threats to himself and his family, real or imagined, and responded with even more oppression. This is the trap that eventually all dictators fall into, even if they have started out with the best of intentions.

Historians sometimes classify Salazar as a "benevolent dictator". There is no such thing. Ask his opponents who languished in his horrific prisons, and ask the thousands of families whose fathers, sons and daughters disappeared.

In the judgement of the Portuguese people, decades after his demise, Salazar is given credit for having modernized government, having kept his country out of WWII and having put its economy back on the road of recovery, slowly but steadily improving the material lives of its people.

But the Portuguese also remember the price they had to pay. Today, they ask themselves - was it all worth the pain, the agony, of thirty six years of oppression?

Spain's Franco

General Francisco Franco had led Spain's ultra-right ("Loyalist") party to victory in the Spanish civil war. He was adored by the Right for his successes as their general, and hated by the left for the atrocities that he condoned in his ruthless military campaigns - but as a result, he was perhaps the best known man in his time in Spain.

Shortly after the war had ended the Spanish Senate appointed him Head of State, in the hope that with his prestige as an eminent military leader he could bring peace to the badly fragmented Spanish political landscape. As it turned out, General Franco found it surprisingly easy to grow into his new role as politician, moving with great speed to take a number of sensible steps to consolidate the new government. From the outset, the Senate had given him some extraordinary powers meant to help him deal swiftly with the country's huge economic and social ills.

Soon the Senate came to regret its generosity. Franco found it difficult to shed a general's deeply ingrained habit of making unilateral decisions - soon he would take on much more authority for himself than the Senate had meant to give him. When the Senate tried to reign him in, he took his case to the ultra-right militia, the 'Falange', who under his orders took to the streets, beating up any opponents and intimidating the courts. The Senate relented.

This is when Franco started to believe that "destiny" was showing him the way to Spain's salvation, that only he understood what really ailed his country, and that only he would know how to fix it - the quintessential belief system of budding dictators. Coupled with his General's mentality he was ready to take over.

As ambitious he was, he did not have the make-up of a demagogue. As an orator, he was average, his speeches uninspiring. He deftly turned this limitation into his advantage by appearing as the calm and collected person, dispassionately and unselfishly having only the interests of his country at heart. Also, he never let people forget that he was a devout church-goer. Behind this image, however, lurked a man without scruples, hard and cynical.

He knew very well that in order to get complete control and to keep on top, he had to create a devoted following that would be ready to support him, no matter what. He knew his Spaniards - he reminded them of their two thousand year history, that at one time Spain ruled much of the world, and that he would make them proud again of their heritage and their country.

To keep the image of the glory of old Spain in front of people at all times he promoted the 'Falange' emblem. It was derived from the Roman insignia of authority, a bundle of arrows arranged over an oxen's yoke, not so subtle as an icon of oppression. To show support for Franco's Spain every one was expected to wear some form of the Falange icon on their clothing. He made his Falange militia wear a military-style cap complete with the tassel and the Falange insignia.

This symbolism had another more insidious aspect: as a private citizen you were expected to wear it all the time to show your support of the regime. The simple act of *not* wearing it was soon seen as a sign of opposition - often with dire consequences. Having to wear the dictator's symbol all the time also resulted in a form of self-reinforcing publicity - an effective way to create a personality cult, the stuff that all dictators love.

Franco told his people over and over that Spain's salvation required unity, and he coined the phrase "Unitary National Identity" to justify his increasingly oppressive rule. Partly to ensure the continued backing of the ultra-right he proceeded with banning all labor unions, out-lawing all political parties and the free press, and replacing judges who had demonstrated independence. Anyone opposing his decrees would wind up in prison, in concentration camps or would simply disappear. For the next twenty eight years he would rule Spain as its undisputed dictator.

But why, after having already achieved almost complete control over his nation did he become such a cruel despot? In the end, and in spite of his outward show of a general's bravado, deep under, Franco was a very insecure person. Knowing that given an opportunity his many enemies would be ready to take him down he developed and intricate system of surveillance, making every one spy on every one else, extracting information on real or imagined plots against him with elaborate torture techniques, in the fine tradition of the Spanish Inquisition. A failed attempt on his life gave him a renewed excuse for 'purging' his real or perceived enemies.

(Irony of history - this particular assassination attempt was performed by an airplane dropping a bomb on Franco, something like a revenge for the infamous bombing attack on the town of Guernica by Franco's forces a few years earlier.)

Nothing was too base for Franco to assure him that he would stay in power - and stay alive. He lived in constant fear that his enemies would deal him the same horrible end of his life as he had so often dealt them.

Small of stature and with unimpressive looks his ego drove him to start an almost pathological personality cult, forcing the schools to teach the children that he had been sent by "Divine Providence'" to save Spain from political chaos and from the people's poverty. But all while proclaiming his devotion to the nation's welfare he would amass a huge fortune for himself and his family - over half a billion dollars worth of real estate and art, mostly expropriated from those he had sent to prison and to death as "Enemies of the Nation".

In addition to his personal cruelty, Franco probably was the most predatory of all modern day dictators. Also, with a general's arrogance, he had only contempt for civilian ways to govern, a base cynic.

How did he get to become such a powerful despot, and how did he manage to stay in absolute power for so long? To become popular with his following he used the slogan "Make Spain Glorious Again" and reinforced it with all the symbolisms he could devise. Once in absolute power he used all the tools of a psychopath - perhaps the dictator with an all-time low as a person.

The Spanish Civil War had cost the lives of 300,000 soldiers. In the years following the war more than 200,000 civilians were murdered by Franco's right-wing militia, victims of their dictator's frantic efforts to stay in power at all cost. They were buried in 2,000 mass graves officially identified and carefully mapped by today's democratic Spanish government.

Today's Spaniards prefer not talk about the Franco era. For those who still remember, it is too painful a subject. In their schools, children are taught that it was an era of much confusion, of Spaniards fighting Spaniards, of political disunity that needed to be ended. Could this have been achieved by means less divisive, less cruel? Was it really necessary to put the country through such agony for eight years of civil war and then thirty six years of oppression by a cruel dictator?

Argentina's Peron

Leaving his military career for politics, Juan Peron became Minister of Labor and then was elected three times as Prime Minister during the Cold War era that had put his country in the middle of Latin America's struggle against communist domination. As Labor Minister, he had made a name for himself as a strong proponent of labor reforms aimed at improving dismal working conditions and inadequate pay, especially for the unskilled farm laborers. As the "common man's president" his motto was "make Argentinians proud again to live here."

Unlike Spain's Franco, Peron had to campaign the regular way for his presidency. He was already well known as an effective (leftist) advocate for labor and thus commanded a built-in lead over his centrist opponents. Then it occurred to him that the usual centrist based government would be bound to fail again because it would always be faced with the two-front battle of the Center against the Left as well as against the Right, which had lead to paralysis several times before.

So he hit upon a brand new way of getting his country to move forward - create a government that would be based on a coalition of the Left with the Right. At first sight this seemed to be an impossible task but with his superb negotiating skills Peron, indeed, got these two opposing camps to work together. It resulted in a coalition of the workers (the Descamisados, 'shirtless') and the establishment Right, especially its military. It would become known widely as the "Peronist Solution"to be emulated by other Latin American countries, however, with mixed results. But it was a shrewd move - with the workers on his side, Peron was assured of their votes, and with the military, if necessary, the force of their arms.

But even more important, Peron had succeeded in transferring his messianic belief in the good future for Argentina to his followers in both of these camps. His followers now were the ones to make sure, by hook or crook, that the other Argentinian political groups would succumb to their will. Peron had succeeded to make himself unassailable.

In his efforts to bring the dispossessed back into the mainstream of national life he got immense help from his wife Evita, soon to become even more popular than her husband. Whether by design or by the sheer force of her radiant personality, a new type of personality cult emerged - that of a "Golden Couple", selflessly nurturing their country back into peace and prosperity.

It worked well for Peron, but the truth was elsewhere - as it became clear much later, Peron was not above enriching himself shamelessly at the expense of his fellow Argentinians.

Anyway, soon Argentina was well on its way to become an orderly country again, recognized widely as the best of Latin America. Not only had Peron succeeded in getting his country going again but his concept of creating a workable government by welding together parts of the left and the right wings would be imitated by other countries and appropriately labeled the 'Peronist' solution. And he had achieved this remarkable feat without using force, to this point.

So why then did Peron start to use strong-arm tactics when he had already achieved his main goal by entirely legal means? Again, the answer is to be found in the seductive nature of a messianic belief that eventually will make a leader simply unable to accept any form of dissent.

After his celebrated success to put the Argentina economy back on a sound footing he fell for the temptation to eliminate anyone who would stand in his way. He had already fired several judges who were not among his supporters, and when his private "security forces" had beaten the editor of an opposition newspaper to death there somehow was no court willing to prosecute the murderers.

Soon after Peron had gotten away with eliminating one opponent without legal consequences, full-scale persecutions were on their way, with thousands incarcerated, tortured hideously and often simply disappearing. The more of this he did, the more it became clear to him that unless he would continue to dominate by sheer force of terror, he would find the the same painful end as he was inflicting on so many others. His first foul deed had started him on a path of ever escalating violence.

After all his initial good work Peron had joined the infamous ranks of dictators - a deplorable ending of an otherwise admirable life of service to his country. In the end, his messianic belief of his own superiority would negate the best of his original intentions and mar his otherwise splendid record as leader who more than most had understood the needs of his people.

With their period of dictatorship way in the past Argentinians now have mixed feelings about Peron. They prefer not to talk about Peron's crimes but that Argentina had emerged from its nightmare a better country, a better society. For many the basic question still is hanging over them whether it was it worth the many years of harsh rule, of street violence, of thousands of people disappearing. Above all, has Argentina learned enough from its years of oppression to make sure that it will never have to succumb to dictatorship again?

Italy's Mussolini

Just like Germany's Hitler, Benito Mussolini had become the head of Italy's democratic government through entirely legitimate means, even though, just like Hitler, he never got more than one third of the popular vote. But this made his party the biggest and under Italy's constitution that gave him the right to form a government. He became Italy's Prime Minister in 1922. Soon he would rule his country as dictator.

But it was not that he was imitating Hitler - it was the other way around. Hitler became Germany's leader a full decade later, and it was actually Hitler who saw Mussolini as his mentor. In fact, they became close personal friends, 'two peas in a pod'.

Of all the European countries, how would Italy ever succumb to a dictator, a country where the idea of enjoyment of life is quintessential, and where individuality always trumps the very idea of following any government rules?

Actually, at the time Mussolini became Prime Minister, Italy was ripe for major changes. Although Italy had been fighting alongside the Allied in the first world war it had been treated badly when the time came to share in the spoils of their victory. Italy's self-esteem was at an all-time low, its government institutions in disarray, its economy in shambles, crushing poverty everywhere.

So, Italy was fertile grounds for massive changes. Four years into having tried hard to make the hopelessly fractured legislative work, Mussolini had the future dictator's epiphany - that only he understood what really was ailing his country, and only he would be able to remedy it. He was ready to take control of the country. But how to do this in a country where blindly following a leader was not considered such a good idea?

Mussolini was uniquely positioned for this task. In his earlier career as newspaper editor he had learned how to phrase stories to make them easily understood by audiences with very different levels of education. In his years in Italy's legislature he became very much aware of the difficulties to get groups with diverse interests come to agreements on anything. Above everything else, however, he saw that Italians of all economic and social levels had lost faith in their own country. Beyond the rampant poverty many Italians were deeply ashamed of their country. Nothing seemed to work - one government after another failing in rapid sequence, infrastructure crumbling, trains almost never on schedule. The country was bankrupt. No wonder so many Italians felt deeply humiliated.

Mussolini knew exactly what to do to get his compatriots out of this state of despair - he dug deep into Italy's glorious past, showing his people how their Roman ancestors once dominated the known world, how they taught discipline to unruly barbarians, how they bestowed laws and civic order to their world. In this vein he resurrected the ancient Roman symbol of authority, the Lictorian Ax and made it the official insignia of his party. It was proudly called the "Fascia", from the latin for "bundle", meaning "everything held together in one", evoking the idea of national unity.

This symbol actually gave his movement its name: "Fascist", and it became the visual emblem of the new Italy. Italians had to wear the icon of Fascism all the time, and they had to display the fascist flag at every occasion. Not to do so would identify them as the 'Enemy of the Nation', with the usual dire consequences. Soon, Mussolini's portrait had to appear everywhere. His personality cult was well on its way.

Next, Mussolini targeted the poor, the dispossessed, and by a flagrant misuse of public money organized them into his private political crack troops, the infamous "Black Shirts". He made them wear a martial looking hat featuring the Lictorian Ax emblem, soon to be adopted by just about every Italian organization - a masterstroke of publicity. At his direction they would roam the streets, beat opponents into submission, and break up opposition meetings. Every one not wearing the new national insignia risked being beaten up by the Black Shirts.

He used his Black Shirts to organize rallies all over the country where he would whip the crowds into a frenzy with his fiery and often bombastic rhetoric, mocking opponents with biting sarcasm, accompanied by often comical theatrics. Like an entertainer, he was thriving on the adoration by the masses, but more important, used his charisma to transfer his messianic belief in a "New Italy" to his followers who then were willing to carry out any of his increasingly oppressive edicts.

After that, Mussolini's transition from Prime Minister to Italy's dictator was easy and almost unavoidable. To his credit his programs to make Italy into a modern country again were hugely successful. The country recovered economically with almost full employment, its infrastructure vastly improved, trains running on time again. On the surface, Italy had come back. But behind the facade of success, Italy was financially bankrupt. Getting the economy going and creating millions of jobs with government money had exhausted its treasury.

Above all, it had come at a huge cost to personal freedom. Every one now depended on the State for a job, for personal security, for access to education. In a way, all this was totally the opposite of what Italians traditionally appreciated so much in their personal lives. How could the Mussolini dictatorship have survived against this background?

It survived for almost twenty years because of increasingly brutal suppression of any opposition. Quite early in his rule, there had been three attempts on his life which he conveniently used as justification for Stalin-like purges, with any legal recourse squelched by the judges beholden to him. Only the agonies of the Second World War would finally make the Italians put an end to their Mussolini disaster, dealing him the same horrible death that he and his henchmen had so often dealt to his growing numbers of enemies. His constant fear had come true that one day the many enemies he had made during his reign of terror would catch up with him.

It would take decades of very slow recovery to overcome his legacies. The jury is still out whether in the end anything good came out of Italy's dictatorship era. But it shows that even in a country with such strong preferences for individual personal liberties, dictatorship can happen if a demagogue succeeds in infecting enough of its people with his messianic bug.

What do Italians now say about their time under Mussolini? For most, all the agony and suffering during his dictatorship seems too far in the past to matter to them very much.

But their recurring comment is that if it could happen in a country as individualist as theirs, it could happen anywhere.

Three

AMERICA
ARE WE
SAFE FROM
DICTATORSHIP?

"There can be no liberty without a free press."
Margret Thatcher, British Prime Minister 1979 to 1990

What is happening to our America?

Emerging from under the ruins of WWII, most of the world was determined to prevent this tragedy from repeating itself ever again. Above all, there was wide consensus among the surviving nations that spreading democracy would be the answer, with the United States spearheading this movement. For many generations, our country's moral leadership was in large measure based on our belief in the superiority of our system of government, especially on the effectiveness of our "Checks and Balances" that would make it impossible for a strongman in the style of Hitler to get in power here.

Until a new wave of American nationalism made Donald Trump our President.

Just like years ago most Germans could not believe that someone like Hitler could become their leader, most Americans could not conceive how a person like Trump could possibly wind up as our President. After all, Trump was a political outsider, with no government experience, with a questionable history as a real estate wheeler-dealer, widely considered a somewhat shady con-artist showman. But somehow he did become our President.

Here is the way he was clawing his way into his presidency:

- Trump used the oratory of a true demagogue, applying all his con-artist tools, lying unabashedly to discredit his opponents.

 - With his crudeness he appealed to many Americans' lowest instincts, whipping up his followers with hateful speeches and raucous rallies.

- With his mottos: "we will make America great again" and "America First!" he seduced many unsuspecting Americans to overlook his deceit and base morals.

- He inflamed his followers with blaming hapless minorities for our country's problems, and by promising to prosecute them without due process, trampled on all the moral values of our Nation.

- Appealing to the sentiments of the extreme Right he promised to tear up international agreements, attacked our judicial institutions and declared our free press the "Enemy of the People".

Does this sound uncomfortably similar to what the Germans heard during their future dictator's election campaign?

But even after a vicious campaign filled with overt lies, with crass bullying and unprecedented personal attacks on his opponents, Trump did not manage to win a majority - just 46.1% of the popular vote, almost ten percentage points less than his opponent. He won the Presidency anyway because our election system's Electoral College over-riding the popular majority.

At first, when all the votes were in, America breathed a sigh of relief to learn that Trump had lost, but that did not last long because the Electoral College made him President anyway. You could see clearly that even Trump was taken by surprise with his body language telling "now what?"

Still, why did so many of us vote for a person like Trump in spite of his glaring faults and his abrasive ways? Was he not known as a habitual liar? Was he not known for his irresponsible rhetoric, for his outlandish personal behavior, his crass sexual exploits? Or was it, perhaps, because many of us secretly admired him for all that?

Does this sound like the leader we want? Is he the leader we deserve? Many Americans were shaking their heads in disbelief, with even more shaking of heads in the rest of the world. How could this have happened in America, of all places, in our country that has such a proud history of democratic government that by and large had attracted men and women of the highest caliber into public office?

Does this perhaps sound like Trump having plans to become an autocrat, a strongman with aspirations to 'rule' the country? Of course, he would vehemently deny it, but the way he conducts himself may tell us how he really sees his leadership. Who knows - Trump may be a very astute student of history after all. The way he acts in his White House, the way he interacts with his support groups seems to following the same pattern we have seen in other autocrats, present and past. He certainly has openly shown his admiration for the strongmen of our days in other nations.

How is it possible for this to happen in our own country, a nation built on many generations of democracy, the envy of much of the world for the freedoms we enjoy?

A most unlikely Coalition of Voters

Much of the world admires America for its long history of political stability, its well-designed institutions, its stature in world affairs, and above all, for the personal freedom it grants its people.

So why then did we elect a President whose programs are aimed at disrupting our domestic political stability, diminishing our institutions, attacking our rights of free expression, confusing our friends abroad while he is sidling up to our foes?

There cannot be any doubt about our President's agenda. He has made that plenty clear in his election campaign and ever since in office. How then do we explain why important groups of voters with well defined needs would vote for a candidate who in so many words had told them that he would act contrary to their interests once in office?

Why would our farmers vote for Trump after he told them that he would tear up the very trade agreements they so much depended upon? Why the poor of Appalachia when he told them that he would repeal 'Obamacare' and other state health care programs they so much depend upon? Why the Evangelicals when his base morals represent everything they say they detest? Why the middle-class suburbanites after Trump has showed his disdain for the value of education, the very basis of their privileged status? Why the military when he set out to damage the very alliances built to help us against our country's foes?

There is nothing new that people sometimes vote against their own interests, when rational thinking makes way to emotions. Wanting to be elected many politicians will try to move people away from uncomfortable facts by arousing their passions with high-sounding slogans, such as "I will make America great again", effectively defusing any voter concerns. As a politician, Trump excels in this technique. But this alone was not what helped him in his quest for power.

Probably more than any other politician, Trump had always been very keenly aware of the huge value of name branding, of drawing attention to himself in everything he was doing. With his outsized ego he founded his candidacy on the image he had so carefully constructed as a man who would stand above the nation's politics and tackle its woes without the restraints of our traditional way of doing things. This, of course, is exactly what dictators all over the world are doing to shield themselves from any possible opposition. Hitler and Franco and Mussolini and all the other dictators of this world had done the same thing very successfully.

Catering to those who felt that they had been left behind, Trump started to make increasingly irresponsible campaign promises. Of course, all politician are quick to make promises, but Trump carried this to such an extreme that even some in his own ranks became concerned.

As he began to act on his campaign promises many Americans were disturbed seeing how he was trying to dismantle our health care, recklessly burdening the nation with huge debts by one-sided tax cuts, tearing up vital international agreements, making long-time allies doubt our commitments, and sidling up to criminal dictators. His defense was very direct: "Look, I told you in my campaign speeches that this is what I would do, and see, I am true to my word - now stop complaining!"

Those of us who were hoping that once in office Trump would simmer down and act like a statesman would be sorely disappointed. We may find it difficult to understand that many important voter groups supported Trump's campaign, somehow believing his unrealistic claims, and somehow willing to overlook his erratic and often insulting behavior.

Now that he had his opportunity to show us and the world what he is really about, why does he still enjoy such a large following even with groups that have already suffered from his ill-advised actions? It seems that instead of "buyers remorse" we see that too many

Americans refuse to admit that having voted him into office was a huge mistake.

Is Trump really sincere when he makes his often outlandish claims, or is he, in his showman mentality, totally unaware how outrageous he appears? Or is he the ultimate cynic, laughing inwardly about how gullible his followers are? Is there any conscience behind his blatant lies, any shame for his clownish behavior? Or is something hiding behind this facade that he does not want us to see, and we may not like to see? Or is it nothing more than a man's desperate efforts to stay ahead of the law for his personal misdeeds and his many law-breaking actions as President.

Maybe we will never know the real Trump, but perhaps what we see is all there is - a bumbling charlatan, void of common morality, a national embarrassment, an easy prey to our wily adversaries. But this does not make him any less dangerous when called upon to deal with our complex national issues and with the world.

But no matter what his real motives, he is shrewdly building up his image as the defender of the 'common man' while through his actions he is doing everything to tilt the economy further in the direction of large corporations and the super-wealthy. His base has become an uncritical block of voters, defending him without giving thought to the fact that they are being used by the man they so adore, for his own selfish purposes.

A devoted and determined base is the dream of every politician. A base which is so enthralled with their leader that it will literally take to the streets to fight for him is the life blood of autocrats. Dictators like Hitler had succeeded in creating huge followings of people who had given up their own thinking in favor of eating up every nonsense that their leader would dish out to them in riotous rallies and in a never ending stream of hateful propaganda. Are the screaming crowds of Trump's rallies any different in their blind compliance with his demagoguery?

Let us not give up hope that we can stop this before it is getting totally out of hand. But just expressing our disdain will not be enough. It will take concerted action by us, the people, that democracy is all about - starting with the ballot box.

The Powers of our President

The office of our President is often referred to as the most powerful one in the entire world.

So much power brings with it a huge responsibility. The person holding such power obviously must be the most responsible of statesman to be sure that it will always be exercised with the utmost of care and restraint.

As the leader of the nation, we look to our President to give us a vision where he wants to take us for a better and more secure future. Some presidents were at their best when they showed us they had succeeded in enlisting all the resources of our government for the benefit of the country and its people, within the powers given to them by our Constitution.

Some of them were at their worst when they used their already vast powers to enlarge them even further, beyond what the Constitution had meant to bestow upon them. As it is in the nature of humans, the more powers we have the more we are tempted to abuse them.

When our Founding Fathers wrote our Constitution over two hundred years ago they were very much afraid of possibly losing the newly won freedom by a relapse into some form of autocracy. To this aim they tried to limit the powers of the President in such a way as to prevent this from happening, ever.

But they also had to take into consideration the realities of their times and the conditions under which the newly formed government had to be made functional. Because at that time the mail would take weeks, and going to meet with other government bodies meant long trips by stage coach, they had to grant the newly established office of the President important powers to enable him to make decisions on his own when there was no time to wait for input from others.

For this reason our Constitution gave the President the power to make unilateral decisions in a number of areas without having to first obtain the concurrence of other parts of the government. As a result, our President can, on his own, make de-facto laws simply by "Executive Orders", like terminate international agreements, change military alliances, impose tariffs on trade, and in his capacity as Commander-in-Chief, even commit our military into action. In our modern times, these communication problems simply no longer exist, and therefor our President should not have the right to make such far reaching decisions on his own. No other modern democracy gives its leaders anywhere near such powers.

As an example, our President's un-paralleled powers allow him to unilaterally impose "sanctions" on other nations. Remember that sanctions are what in times past were called "blockades", which were often considered to be tantamount to a declaration of war. Is Trump aware what he might be precipitating with his poorly-thought out sanctions? How are we going to deal with friendly nations when it will come to enforcing our sanctions?

Of course, he is constitutionally obligated to seek after-the-fact congressional approval for his unilateral decisions, but does he really do it? And what, in practice, can be done when he doesn't, and when his unilateral actions have already created a new set of realities? And is all this in keeping with what our country believes to be legitimate, and what our Founding Fathers wanted?

It seems there is a substantial difference in what our President believes to be his prerogatives and what most of us believe the Constitution meant to give him. By any standards such powers given to a single person seem way out of line with today's needs. In the hands of someone with less than wise restraint they are potentially very dangerous.

To add to this controversy, Trump now keeps saying that our judiciary has no right to apply its rules of investigation to him, that perhaps he could even pardon himself if accused (or convicted?) of anything. This comes down to the question of whether our President is, de facto, above the Law.

Just the fact alone that our President is talking about these matters should alert us to the likelihood that he, indeed, believes that he does have these extraordinary rights. Should we simply accept our President's interpretation of his constitutional rights without questing his ultimate motives?

Our Constitution - timeless or not?

There are those who like to tell us that our Constitution must not, under any circumstances, be altered, that it must remain the eternal bedrock of our political life, and that we should always take it literally as originally written. These same people, however, conveniently ignore that we have already seen it altered *twenty-seven times* in response to our nation's changing needs. Like all government rules, those provisions of our Constitution that were solely addressing the unique conditions of 230 years ago need to be up-dated with the changing life conditions of our Nation.

Take for example, the institution of our 'Electoral College'. It was established some 230 years ago, to appease some of our Founding Fathers who were still deeply distrustful of the concept of direct popular voting for President. As the 'Elitists' they were, many of them still had great reservations about entrusting so much voting power to the common man. Their argument was also based on the fact that at that time many, if not most, Americans were illiterate and thus limited in their ability to inform themselves about government matters.

They were also trying to deal with the problems of communications and travel, but certainly none of those reasons are valid today. There simply is no reason to hold on to the Electoral College. Of course, the politicians who owe their ascent to power to this strange construct have no interest to do away with it. That is the reason, probably the only real reason, why we still have it.

But we should not just shrug our shoulders and live with it because it has a dangerous component for the very existence of our democracy - it puts doubts into the legitimacy of our presidential elections when the Electors over-rule a popular majority vote. In fact, the power of this Electoral College is such that it is entirely possible that one day it will put into our highest office some one who has no legitimate claim at all.

The other area of grave concern is the way we choose our senators. Our Founding Fathers, composed mainly of the Colonies' new aristocracy meant the Senate to be an 'elitist' body - its governing motto attests to that idea: "Advise and Consent". They thought of it as a counter-balance to the House which they viewed as representing the 'masses'. Also, when they created the Senate 230 years ago our Founding Fathers decided that each of the thirteen colonies would have the same number of senators (two) so that each colony would have an equal say regardless of its population size.

But at that time the differences in population between the bigger and the smaller colonies were not anywhere near as large as they are now. Today our five most populous states account for over 38% of the US population but they have the same number of senators (20) as the bottom five that *together* account for not even one percent of our country's population. This gross imbalance could be very dangerous to our democracy as the smaller states' senators can practically dominate the Senate's decision making process. It is the opposite of the basic democratic concept of "equal representation".

No way could the writers of our Constitution have foreseen that their decision on the Senate's make-up would one day lead to an intolerably lop-sided composition that is undoubtedly far away from their original intent. It stands to reason that had our Founding Fathers seen anywhere near such huge population differences they would have undoubtedly instituted a more equitable way to apportion Senate seats. This is a clear case where over the past 230 years our country's sets of circumstance have changed so much, giving ample justification for yet another Amendment - no way can it be argued that the Founding Fathers' original thought process should be applied to population facts that are now vastly different.

In the present constellation the senators from our low population states, if banded together, are in a position where they could over-ride anything our House of

Representatives may decide, just because they can - in fact, they often do. They can legitimize just about everything our President and his Executive Branch are doing - and they are already doing so. They are creating a clear path for some one to grab more power than we, the people, would be willing to bestow. For example, with its lop-sided composition, our Senate has been able to push through judicial appointees who are clearly beholden to our President and his Party's philosophy - in step with our current administration's efforts to dismantle the independence of our judiciary branch.

Obviously, our country's situation and needs are different from those 230 years ago. Amendments to our Constitution to bring it in line with today's national requirements are sorely needed. We have made quite a few changes to our Constitution as new circumstances arose - *twenty-seven times*. It is unrealistic to argue otherwise just to avoid changes simply because they could limit the powers of politicians who owe their positions to those outdated provisions.

It is difficult to make these needed changes because the very senators who would be asked to make them are the same men and women who so greatly benefitted from these absurd antiquated arrangements. It would take true statesmanship instead of the narrow focus on their own personal advantages that unfortunately is now so pervasive in our government institutions. One could say that there is a flaw in our procedural set-up. Let us hope that flaws like this will not become lethal to our democracy.

The good news is that the founders of our Nation firmly established at least one truly everlasting and sound government principle - our system of "Checks and Balances". This ingenious system establishes our three government branches to be free from domination by any one of them. Some try to justify our President's abnormal powers by pointing to the sad fact that our Legislative, our Congress, is in a seemingly perpetual stage of paralysis, and that in order to get anything done our President just has no choice but to by-pass it with his flood of 'Executive Orders'. But where will such an attitude lead us? Is this not opening the doors to a more autocratic way of governing? Are we already accepting this undemocratic way as the "new norm?"

If we let it happen that our Executive Branch takes on more and more decision making on its own, then the very basic concept of our Constitution is being challenged, and it will be changed not by thoughtful deliberation and well reasoned amendments, but by default alone. Is that what we would like to see happen?

This hollowing-out of one part of our government structure for the benefit of the Executive is also happening right now in a number of otherwise modern countries, even among our Allies, like Poland, Hungary, Turkey and then, of course, Russia. We are justly worried that as those countries already are de facto ruled as autocracies, they may sooner or later turn into full-fledged dictatorships. We have seen this pattern before - what starts as seemingly 'constructive' executive decision-making can easily lead to more and more autocracy. From there, the step into dictatorship is not a very big one.

It is disconcerting that our President chooses to be more friendly with the would-be dictators in these countries than with our traditional democratic allies. By showing them so much admiration, does that indicate that Trump, too, would love to rule like they do? When China's President Xi Jinping made himself its leader for life, Trump commented "...maybe one day we should try that, too".

It would certainly be the opposite of what most Americans would want, but are we doing enough to stem this tide?

The Case for an Independent Judiciary

A truly independent judiciary is the most important guarantee for our freedoms.

In all modern societies there are three opposing forces to be kept in balance - the natural force aiming at maximizing personal freedom, the need of society to safeguard its interests, and for government to assert its authority. The judiciary's function is to keep these opposing interests in an often delicate balance.

When the judiciary fails to do its job impartially, or is kept from doing it altogether, society breaks down, with either anarchy leading to chaos, or dictatorship leading to oppression.

We all want an independent and impartial judiciary, but what are we actually doing to make sure that we in fact have one?

The first thing, of course, is to put good laws on the books, but these are only as good as the judges who interpret and then apply them.

So, a good part of having an independent and impartial system of justice depends on how we select our judges.

For reasons to be found in the rural history of our country, we Americans have established that we elect our judges by citizens' vote. It is a valid question whether in this day and age this is still a good way - but this is what we still do. In most modern democracies, in order to eliminate the undue influence of politics or ideology, judges are not elected by public vote but appointed by panels of fellow jurists. For example, in England, judges are selected by the "Judicial Appointment Commission" which is a strictly non-political body composed of jurists appointed in turn by England's equivalent of our American Bar Association.

This very question comes to the fore when we put judges on our Supreme Court, our court of last resort, where fundamental issues of law and of our society are being deliberated and decided.

In our system, our Supreme Judges are nominated by our President. Every president who is given an opportunity to fill a Court vacancy will, naturally, try to find a judge who most likely will side with him in his decision making, thus trying to 'stack' the Court in his favor. His nominee will then be vetted by Congress and, hopefully, then approved, mostly along party lines. By definition, this means the process by which we appoint our Supreme Judges is essentially a political one, not one limited to considerations of jurisprudence.

Thus, inevitably, the decisions about a Supreme Judge will be made not just on the basis of his credentials as a jurist but on how he will support a particular ideology or party platform. Is that a good thing, and is that what we, the citizens, really want? It is hard to imagine that this is what our Founding Fathers wanted.

'Stacking' of our courts has been done many times. Of course, it is something that should not be done. It remains somewhat tolerable as long in the vetting process a good amount of weight is given to the ability of the candidate *as jurist*. The habit of stacking a court becomes onerous when the candidate's ideological orientation becomes the deciding factor.

This has happened before. Both our Parties have, at times, been culprits in forcing this issue, probably to the detriment of our society's trust in this exalted institution. In the past few years, however, the stacking of our Court has been driven almost entirely in the direction of ideology.

One recent flagrant case occurred when the Republican congress refused to consider President Obama's eminently qualified Court nominee under the pretext of the "up-coming" election (at that time almost one whole year away) just so that they could bring in their own candidate later who, predictably, was clearly a choice based on ideology.

Throughout his campaign, Trump emphatically stated that he would only nominate judges who would be supporting his agenda, especially on racial and gender equality, women's choice, and health care. Given these openly stated criteria, how could any one say that the jurists who Trump then nominated would be impartial?

By stacking the Court with judges along the lines of ideology, the Court is now set not just to *interpret* the Law, which is what a court should do, but to in fact *legislate from the bench*. Thus, our Supreme Court is becoming just another political body meant to do the President's bidding.

The result is that Trump can now effectively rule the country by "Executive Order", assured that our Supreme Court will in all likelihood put its rubber stamp of approval on just about everything our President wants to do.

Trump has, in effect, done away with our time-honored system where Congress, not the Judiciary, is the one to make the laws.

Selecting our Supreme Courts justices on the basis of their personal beliefs and ideologies is an insidious attack on the integrity of our judicial system. Should we not be concerned about how far we have already gone away from our reliance on the Constitution and its "Checks and Balances"?

Looking back at Germany's descent into dictatorship, Hitler's first step was to stack the German courts with judges who would be ready to do his bidding. It ended the independence of its judicial system. Look what this has done to Germany, and to world peace!

Do we want this for our country?

Truth or Consequences?

"The liberty of the press is indeed essential to the nature of a free state."
(William Blackstone, British jurist and statesman, 1765)

Our American way of life is best explained by our deep conviction that our personal liberties are fundamental to our existence as a Nation. Nothing will shake us more than any attempt to tamper with our liberties, our personal freedoms, especially our right of free expression.

But are we really guarding these freedoms with all our hearts as we always like to assert?

Our freedom of expression is enshrined in our Constitution's First Amendment. Its language is crystal clear and requires no special interpretation - and yet our leaders every so often like to ignore it whenever it suits their particular purposes. It has periodically turned into a 'tug of war' between government which often prefers to push back on uncomfortable publicity, and on our sources of public information, the 'media'.

Under President Trump, this discord has reached new heights, culminating in Trump repeatedly declaring the media "the enemy of the people". The world has heard this phrase many times before - used over and over by autocrats and dictators. Most of us will agree that we have never expected to hear it from our very own political leaders. What is happening to us?

The starting point for this new attack on our right of freedom of expression was our President's unfortunate habit of lying - lying shamelessly even when the truth is obvious.

There even is some entirely new vocabulary for the barrage of lies - such as "alternate facts", and "fake news", or the ultimate Orwellian "what you are seeing and what you are hearing is not what is happening."

For many Americans it is hard to understand why our President and his administration would stoop so low with their lying and misrepresentations of the facts even when they are so easily unmasked. And predictably, just because the real truth is so easily found, our President and his administration are bearing down hard on our media.

Where is all this going? Perhaps nothing further will come of it. Maybe we will just become numb to the constant flow of lies and contradictions. But is this not already pretty bad?

Or it may get much worse. We may soon come to a point where we no longer know what to believe about what our President and our government is telling us. Trump's relentless "the media is the enemy of the people" has already become set in the minds of his followers. Just see Trump's rally crowds react to his tirades about our media. The steps from there to 'information control' are not very big ones - we already have witnessed the exclusion of reporters who had dared to ask uncomfortable questions in White House press conferences.

Aspiring dictators know they need to take control of the media before they can subdue their people. Is this what we see happening?

Of course, we are still far away from information control, from censorship, and from declaring some forms of publications illegal. But when will we reach the point when ordinary citizens or government employees will begin hesitating to voice their opinions for fear of being reprimanded, for fear of being removed from their positions?

Dictators fear nothing more than free expression of their citizens' opinions, especially when they are calling out crimes and oppression. To many of us, it may seem far fetched that we may ever see this extreme happen to us here in America. In the beginning, people who had to live through dictatorships in other countries did not want to believe it either. Hitler's Germany did not, either, until one step at a time, its freedom to express their opinions had disappeared.

Could it happen to us here? Let us hope not. But let us also be vigilant. Dictatorships do not always happen overnight - often it is a slow step by step process, coming to us by stealth.

The Dignity of the Office

The forty-four presidents before Trump were very different types of personalities, with very diverse social backgrounds and levels of education. As you would expect from such a broad sample of ambitious men, all came to office with varying degrees of honesty and integrity.

But whatever their unique dispositions, all of them were striving to lend some level of dignity to their high office. All of them would take liberties from time to time with the truth when they felt it would further their ambitions, but they were ashamed or at least uncomfortable when they were called out for their lies.

Each one of them had big egos and wanted to be treated with deference, but most of them would give credit to others when due. They might, at one time or another, have wanted to be liked by the public for their personal traits but none really did too much to push himself forward in this vein.

Every one of them had their flaws, some more than others. Some were not liked for what they did, some were liked for perhaps the wrong reasons. However, all of them commanded respect, not only from their own citizens, but also from other nations. By and large, as Presidents of our country, they made Americans proud.

But then came Trump.

Trump is unlike any other president before him:

Where others cultivated friends, Trump seems to delight in confusing them with falsehoods.

Where others have carefully studied the ways of their foes, Trump ignores advise and likes to rely on his instincts.

Where others made great efforts to build foreign alliances, Trump seems to like breaking them apart.

Where others have communicated with us about their visions for the country in terms that were both sober and understandable, Trump obfuscates with his meandering and his litany of untruths.

Who then is Trump, really?

He likes to describe himself in many different ways - as a hugely successful real estate tycoon, as a famous television actor and producer, as a dealmaker who knows to get whatever he wants by his superior negotiating skills, even calling himself a "stable genius".

This is what he says about himself, but what do others say about him? What is the reality behind this strange man? How did he even manage to become a candidate for our highest office when he had never been in politics, and how did he get elected as our Nation's leader when he never showed himself in a statesman-like manner?

With the benefit of hindsight it has now become quite clear that he has actually been preparing to enter the national political arena for a very long time, but certainly not in the way any other aspiring politician would have done it.

As Trump sees it, studying political history or the workings of government would be a waste of his time. What Trump did instead was what he knows best - promoting his persona to the public, using his television show experience to 'brand' himself as an overpowering 'alpha male'. Bragging about his sexual aggressions and his habitual bullying fits right into the image he was creating for himself.

This was the Trump that entered the presidential race with the bravado that would capture the admiration of certain segments of our population - and the immediate disdain from the rest. Unabashedly divisive, this is how he would forge ahead, seemingly unconcerned with all the wreckages in his wake.

Then he became a typical politician, making grand campaign promises, each one carefully designed to lure specific populations into his camp. No promise too outlandish, nothing that he would not tear down or make new, everything to please one voter group or another. Honed in many years in television, his clownish showmanship came in handy in getting his points across to even the simplest minds.

But he went right to work to put his own stamp on how he thought he would "run America", as he put it. He soon was to discover that it was not going to be that easy.

In his experience as businessman and in television he succeeded with his impulsive and seat-of-his-pants management style. As president, however, decisions also involve other parts of the government, and whatever happens there will be scrutinized in the country's news cycle. It became clear very quickly that Trump did not know how to deal with this - after all he had never served in any public office.

He found his own way by using Twitter to by-pass the regular workings of government and to 'communicate' directly with the people. Hardly a day would pass without Trump telling the country and the world about new policies, new projects, new appointments, and often his own advisors would learn about his statements only from his Tweets.

So many of his Tweets were overt lies, especially when he made erratic statements about policy and the inner workings of the White House. First, many Americans were embarrassed for their newly elected leader. It soon turned out that Trump himself did not show embarrassment but defiance.

Psychologists say that when people are lying often, they not only diminish their credibility in the eyes of others, but they, too, become confused. A liar needs to have an excellent memory - it gets to be very exhausting trying not to get tripped up by too many falsehoods.

Psychiatrists are concerned about the mental health of people who are lying so much that they might actually lose their sense of reality, one step down the path to mental illness. Where does Trump fit in this spectrum?

But in the mind set of his supporters, Trump can do no wrong. No matter how transparent Trump's lies, no matter how often he messes up the workings of government, his supporters keep adoring him. They think his meandering rhetoric is interesting, they gloss over his non-sequiturs, find his clowning lovable, his mocking hilarious, and his failures always someone else's fault. For his adoring followers he has become their "entertainer-in-chief" but this does nothing to keep the Nation informed of what is really going on.

In the meantime Trump supporters are doing their best to help him create his very own personality cult. Trump may not be very interested in learning from history, but he certainly has been good at emulating the time-honored ways of dictators to make themselves unassailable by creating their carefully crafted personality cults.

It is hard to understand why a man like Trump who has shown himself a shrewd operator throughout his life, would want to expose himself to the world's ridicule and disdain about his flagrant lying, his loudmouth attacks on the press, his insulting the leaders of friendly nations, his clowning at rallies. Does this make any sense?

Is it perhaps that all this lying, all this flailing around with the press, tangling with our Allies, conducting secretive meetings, is a part of a plan? Is it perhaps that Trump is going through all these gyrations as part of a cunning scheme to confuse, to divert people's attention away from issues, or is it to hide something? Is it a gigantic scheme for Trump to market himself, to get his name into the news so much that he can overwhelm all opposition with the great advantage of unprecedented name recognition.

But how in all these theatrics are the interests of the Nation taken care of? If all this is done just to feed his insatiable ego, who will attend to our country's pressing needs, who is doing the governing? Is all this done, perhaps, just to hide a big agenda that we are not aware of?

Probably not. In spite of his strange ways, Trump will simply be Trump - a man of unbound ambition, an easy target for flattery, emotionally unstable and without scruples. He may wish to be able to 'rule' the country without the restraints of our governmental set-up, but this is not possible as long as our "Checks and Balances" are still operational.

As long as they are. Couple that with our President's relentless attacks on our freedom of expression and there could be the makings of an increasingly authoritarian way for us to be governed.

The Lure of the 'Great Economy' - once again.

In their quest for votes, every politician will say that he is the one to make the economy better, that he is the one who will create jobs, that he is the one to protect us from the evils of foreign competition.

In a democracy, the ability for any given politician to directly influence our economic fortunes is limited. Even when backed by legislative majorities, there are many constraints - legal as well as financial. Under both Republican and Democrat presidencies there were good economic times and bad ones. More recently the Republicans under Bush's presidency did poorly, running up huge deficits, mostly to pay for ill-conceived wars, pushing badly timed tax cuts and allowing our banks to squander our money. The deep recession that followed wiped out much of our middle class and many, many jobs.

Under the previous administration, the Democrats worked hard to righten the tattered economy, and with a number of quite well thought-out measures succeeded in turning the economy around, put people back to work and stabilized our financial institutions.

We started to extricate ourselves from the Bush era wars, step by step, and even managed to reduce our national deficits.

Of course, all politicians are quick to take credit when things go well, and equally quick to dish out blame when they are not. Trump is no different in this respect but he is setting new records about the speed with which he claims victory on the economics front. It has its intended effect - Trump's followers are already talking about "the good Trump economy" conveniently ignoring the fact that Trump most certainly has little to do with it. But, Ok, we all should be glad that our economy continues to grow. More people have jobs, wages are, very slowly, inching up, stocks are soaring.

But then Trump created new problems for our economy with ill-thought out punitive tariffs and trade restrictions. Many seasoned analysts have tried to figure out what Trump was thinking when he precipitated his trade wars. He said "......trade wars are good and easy to win" when all the experts all over the world had concluded that in sum total trade wars always lead to losses everywhere, and often cause irreparable damage, especially to those who started them.

Trump was soon to find out that slamming tariffs on targeted nations (some of them our closest allies) would back-fire, bringing about the usual unintended consequences and then, retaliation, in a tit-for-tat fashion. So, when his friends the soybean farmers found out that Trump's tariff wars cut into their livelihood, he quickly gave them subsidies *to the tune of $12 billion dollars* to make up for their 'losses' .

Perhaps in this case we should give Trump credit for a quick recovery from the tariff blunder that could have cost him the farmers' votes. He cleverly turned it right around and made their votes even more secure with his $12 billion dollar bribe. Never mind that we tax payers are going to be the ones to foot the bill for his grandiosity.

Is there a pattern here? Trump takes some ill-conceived action which winds up hurting some voter groups, and then he turns around bailing them out with some form of subsidies - and declaring victory. Some voters love it. Taxpayers are not amused.

The main objective for these new uncalled-for tax cuts was to create a boost to the economy and to mitigate the adverse effects of the Trump trade wars. To some extent, it worked, as designed, but the working men and women did not see much benefit for themselves. It turned out that corporations, the biggest beneficiary of the Trump tax cuts, used their windfalls not for investments or new jobs or raising wages but for huge stock buy-back programs which drove up the stock markets, for the benefit of the investor class. It is one 'achievement' for Trump to brag about.

That made some of Trump's base happy, but at what price? Do people realize that the Trump tax cuts will create humongous government deficits and increase our country's indebtedness by over one trillion dollars?

Why would anyone with a sense of responsibility do this to our country?

It is because Trump and his Republican supporters want to make sure that the economy remains good - at least up to election time. They are counting on many of us to 'vote our wallet' and not necessarily the other issues even when these may be of great significance in the long run, like education, health care, or protection of the environment. Trump and his Republicans are ever mindful of the old truism: "It's the economy, stupid!" Trump's Republicans want as many voters as possible to enter the voting booth imbued with the idea of the "good Trump economy".

What Trump and his followers are doing to our country is not something new in the long history of a small group trying to impose their will on a nation. In their days Germans were made to believe that Hitler had created an economic miracle 'making Germany great again'. In reality, Hitler had created short-term prosperity by lavishing money on programs aimed at keeping his followers happy, foremost the military, in their quest to prepare for war. His one-sided economics program helped Hitler keeping control over his nation but it would eventually bankrupt the country and lead it into utter disaster.

In the end, the Trump economics program, coupled with his tax cuts, is not much different. It will increase our country's indebtedness to dangerous levels never seen before in our history. Eventually, our country's insane debts will become due. Who is going to pay the bill with nothing left in our country's treasury? Will we end up just like Hitler's Germany, in bankruptcy, and will it cause us to take similarly desperate measures?

Maybe this time-honored type of voter manipulation will work once again to ensure the continuation of the Trump administration, but it is mortgaging our country's future. It puts our President's personal ambitions to perpetuate his presidency above our country's interests, above the urgent need for modernization of our infrastructure, of our education system, of our social safety nets and a more equitable distribution of our wealth.

It is not what a leader should do to his country. If he does, he is not the great patriot he claims to be.

Epilogue

The ancient Greeks had invented democracy as a way to live in freedom, pushing back despotism that had been the accepted political structure for centuries.

Ever since then people everywhere have been in a never ending struggle trying to defend their natural longing to live in freedom against those who want to dominate them. In our own times, the parties in this perpetual fight are the modern democracies on one side and the dictatorships on the other, with all kinds of variations of autocracies in between.

Where in this spectrum of political systems are we? Are we heading into a direction of a better democracy, or are we heading in the other direction, into a more authoritarian one? What are the directions we see in our present leaders, in our President?

We Americans believe that we are secure in our democratic ways, in our freedoms. Most of us have faith in the decency of our compatriots and in the basic fairness of our political system, and these beliefs give us justification to hope that our country will not ever veer off into an authoritarian form of government.

147

This faith in the stability of our government concept, however, should not lead us into complacency. We need to be vigilant and act decisively at the first signs of our politicians grabbing more power than we are comfortable giving them.

Are we comfortable with President Trump's ways? Are we comfortable with his attacks on our right to freely express our opinions? Are we comfortable with his bungling our relations with other nations? Are we comfortable with his undermining the independence of our judiciary? Do we know, really, where he is heading?

No one likes to make comparisons between the way he tries to force his will on our nation and the ways of dictators like Germany's Hitler. But even the most ardent Trump supporters will have to admit that in some areas there are early signs of disturbing similarities.

Trump, of course, would vehemently deny any such parallels. Even when he acts the 'super-nationalist', even after having whipped his followers into a frenzy in his riotous rallies, he never *said* that he was aiming to rule as an autocrat. But in so many of his actions he shows clearly that this is what he, in fact, would love to do. After all, he has brushed aside Congress, set out to discredit our judiciary, openly labeling our free press "the enemy of the people", all telling us what his mind is really set on. He has not established any such thing as a dictatorship, of course, but he could be well on his way to cause us to slide into one - simply because we have so easily become accustomed to glaringly un-democratic ways as the 'new normal'. Is there still time to stop this ominous trend?

It certainly would not be easy. His shrewd use of his talent at showmanship and his 'cheap-shot' orations have served him well in assembling very diverse groups of devoted followers, ready to do his bidding. In his mass rallies he is whipping them into a frenzy. How much more is needed before many will be ready to hit the streets to frighten people into compliance, in the fashion of Mussolini's Black Shirts or Hitler's Brown Militia?

These groups' uncritical embrace of Trump's irresponsible behavior tell us that a new Trump personality cult has already taken hold in our political landscape, not unlike the cult that dictators elsewhere had built around themselves. It is up to the American voters to nudge our leaders back to our true American ways.

Whoever will eventually succeed Trump will have to work hard to set the course for our country back to a better democracy, and not further down the path to a more authoritarian one. Much will depend on our ability to keep our time-honored "Checks and Balances" functioning as they were conceived - with the three branches of our government being equally strong.

To that end, Congress must take back its legislative authority, and our Judiciary needs to dial back its growing politicization. The way to get there is through our voting. It is not just something we *should* do - we *must* do it. This is what our democracy is based on. We will lose it if we do not do our duty as responsible citizens.

Perhaps reading my own very personal account may help you to imagine what it really would be like to live under a dictatorship. Dictatorship is not pretty - there is nothing romantic about it. Even its most arousing mass rallies cannot erase the deep despair that comes from oppression.

And always remember that it is easy for nations to imperceptibly slide into some form of dictatorship but it is almost impossible to get out from under it.

About the Author

Growing up in Nazi Germany he witnessed his country's slide into the nightmare of a dictatorship the likes of which the world had never seen. After barely surviving the war he studied engineering and economics in Germany and Austria, and under a post-graduate Fulbright scholarship in the US, settling eventually here with his young family.

Wolfgang Mack has managed industrial enterprises here, as well as in some countries when they were still reeling under dictatorships. Working closely with their professionals under often trying circumstances gave him a good understanding what it means for ordinary people to live under a dictatorship.

Later, representing industry associations in our halls of politicians and lawmakers he also gained insight in the ways interest groups influence public policy making. He has lectured on these subjects and served on several business and non-profit boards.

He now lives in Seattle, Washington, married to his wife Francesca for more than fifty years, enjoying their four sons and their families, and above all their eleven grandchildren who give special meaning to their lives.